FATS WALLER

His Life and Times

Joel Vance

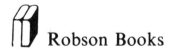 Robson Books

First published in Great Britain in 1979 by
Robson Books Ltd, Bolsover House, 5-6
Clipstone Street, London W1P 7EB.
This Robson paperback edition first published
1992

**British Library Cataloguing-in-Publication
Data**
**A catalogue record for this book is available
from the British Library**

ISBN 0-86051-799-3 (pbk)

Printed in Hungary

1784

to Christopher
el papacito de mi corazon

Contents

Acknowledgments   *vii*

1 Abide with Me   *1*
2 Stayin' at Home   *11*
3 Lost Love   *21*
4 Numb Fumblin'   *29*
5 Goin' About   *37*
6 Soothin' Syrup Stomp   *45*
7 Keepin' Out of Mischief Now   *55*
8 Never Heard of Such Stuff   *65*
9 In Harlem's Araby   *71*
10 Radio Papa, Broadcastin' Mama   *79*
11 That Rhythm Man   *93*
12 Fractious Fingering   *103*
13 London Suite   *115*
14 Slightly Less Than Wonderful   *127*
15 The Jackpot   *143*
16 The Call   *165*
Bibliography   *171*
Index   *173*

Acknowledgments

I must especially thank Mike Lipskin, stride pianist extraordinaire (he was a protégé of Willie "The Lion" Smith), for his advice and encouragement, and for critiquing the manuscript of the book. He is extremely knowledgeable about Waller's and Johnson's era, not only for its music, but for the realities of the recording industry and music publishing companies of that time. The hours I have spent listening to and viewing his remarkable collection of recordings and Waller/Johnson memorabilia have been all the more pleasant for Mike's company. Since we have both experienced the duality of simultaneously being musicians as well as practitioners in the commercial music industry (he as a record producer and I as a press operative), our acquaintance soon became a friendship, which is perhaps the most valuable prize I have gained from the writing of this book. In reviewing the manuscript, he pointed out errors of fact that I have corrected, but I must assume the responsibility for the interpretation of Waller's music, character, and life.

Ms. Elaine Markson, my literary agent, was, as always, resolute in and devoted to my interests. Mr. Ted Williams of AS-CAP kindly provided me with valuable material on Waller and

Johnson from the ASCAP archives (here again, the conclusions I have drawn from material are my own). Mr. George T. Simon located a copy of the 1966 Nash article on Waller, and Mr. Gary Giddons sent me reproductions of rare early Waller newspaper interviews and items.

Mr. Peter J. Davis of the New York *Times* and Mr. Ernest Leogrande of the New York *Daily News* gave me access to the "morgue" files of those journals. Mr. Bill Challis recalled his experiences with Fletcher Henderson and Bix Beiderbecke. Mr. Earl Hines, the amazing and titanic jazz pianist, reminisced about his friendship with Waller in a 1973 interview.

That sublime institution, the New York Public Library, specifically the Library of the Performing Arts at Lincoln Center, contains remarkable archive material on Waller, especially newspaper interviews.

Ms. Muriel Ratner and Mr. Benn Greenspan both allowed me to make use of time that should have been spent in their service for time on the book. Mr. James Goodfriend, music editor of *Stereo Review* magazine, and Dr. Marvin Linick, a gentleman who delights in the accomplishments of his friends, both gave faith and counsel.

J. V.

FATS
WALLER

1
Abide with Me

A DERBY HAT, a jug of gin, and wow. A Cheshire cat grin, a rogue's eyebrows, and a bride's big eyes. A sensuous man who gloried in the delights of food, drink, and company. A manly child. Irresponsible and dedicated, he was never the death of anyone except himself.

A rollicking, roaring performer, he typified "swing" jazz in the 1930s and early 1940s. He could make a song and the piano couple as the act of love. Master of the pop song, he was trained in the classics and preferred the pipe organ. One of the great companions of the twentieth century, whose talk, walk, and charm were artistry in themselves, he was also a serious musician and composer.

Thomas Wright "Fats" Waller got a lot done in his thirty-nine years. He was one of the first black performers to have a regular radio series, to write a complete score for a white stage musical, to give a solo recital at Carnegie Hall. He wrote the music for half a dozen pop tunes that can stand with the best of Harold Arlen, George Gershwin, and Cole Porter: *Ain't Misbehavin'; Honeysuckle Rose; Black and Blue; I've Got a Feeling I'm Falling; Blue, Turning Gray over You; Squeeze Me.*

In a flat declaration made in 1936, "I am the finest jazz organist now alive," Waller was actually being modest. Though he won his fame as a master of the "stride" piano, a two-fisted style that was also capable of great delicacy, Waller virtually invented the organ as a jazz instrument. He was always happiest with it, from his teenage days earning $25 a week as house musician for Harlem's Lincoln movie theater (where he devilishly played *Squeeze Me* one night to accompany a silent newsreel showing the burial of a French general) to the last days of his life, when he earned $72,000 a year as a star of records, radio, personal appearances, and the movies. One of his last recordings was his moving version of the old hymn *Sometimes I Feel like a Motherless Child,* which he interrupted only once to say his famous line: "I wonder what the poor people are doin' tonight. I'd love to be doin' it with 'em!"—a line he had first used in the 1920s when he played for millionaires' private parties.

Waller's humor was even more legendary than his musical prowess. Fat men are generally supposed to be jolly, especially in show business, but Waller had a near-surrealist wit which he used most often to burlesque the lyrics of the many codfish-cake pop songs he recorded. It got quite involved, with Waller sometimes doing several voices and holding dialogues with himself, or suddenly injecting a terribly West Indies accent.

' There are many wonderful Waller lines. In *Stormy Weather,* the 1943 all-black film in which he starred shortly before his death, he plays piano while Ada Brown sings a complaining blues about Fats' ne'er-do-well ways, to which he replies: "Beef to me, baby, beef to me—I don't like pork nohow." A few verses later, while Miss Brown is in the throes of woe, Waller harrumphs: "Suffer, excess baggage, suffer."

On *Draggin' My Heart Around,* which he cut in 1932, Waller sings the cosmopolitan lyrics pretty much straight but cannot resist making his solo a little flowery and saying, "Listen, baby, can't dem trills bring you back to meee?"

Once, during a stage show, a beautiful chorine undulated across the boards, and he called out, "You know what that is? That's that fine Arabian stuff that your dreams is made of," while a bulky comedienne received the comment: "Look at all that meat and no potatoes!" Waller's ribald humor was involved in a wartime salvage program, citizens being urged to sort through their garbage and save any bits of wood, rubber, or tin that could be reprocessed, with the government offering a financial reward. Fats had a song called *Get Some Cash for Your Trash* that Washington thought would be a dandy jingle; the government promoted the song eagerly until it found out what "trash" meant in Harlem slang.

Your Feet's Too Big, a great novelty tune Waller recorded in 1939, contained his most famous line. At the end of the song he interpolated: "Your pedal extremities really are obnoxious. One never knows, do one?"

The American Society of Composers, Authors, and Publishers (ASCAP), which at one time was the collection agency for the works of its "proper" clubhouse members, went before Congress in the middle thirties, seeking a repeal of the old Copyright Law of 1909, which ASCAP rightly claimed was archaic. The general manager of ASCAP complained that a Waller tune, *Flat Tire Papa, Mama's Gonna Give Him Air,* received the same royalty rate as the huff-puff brass band marches of John Philip Sousa. Advised of this, Waller replied:

Do those Congress people feel I am not as good an artist somehow as Mr. Sousa? Why, they're crazy. I have always been an admirer, so to speak, of Mr. Sousa's work. Of course, it isn't jazz, but it's all right for that kind of stuff. To tell you the truth, I had an idea I would put that tune of his, *The Stars and Stripes Forever,* to swing. If they mess around with me, though, I won't do it, I just won't do it. I sure wish they would ask me to testify. I'd rather testify than eat.

The last was a serious statement to make, since Waller loved food, as his 285 pounds witnessed. He once told an interviewer: "No, sir, I never ran away from home—there was too much good food on that table." He also had a heroic drinking capacity, possibly matched only by that of the actor John Barrymore and the statesman Winston Churchill. Waller was able to put away two fifths a day; he favored Old Grandad bourbon, which he called "Grandfather."

Though his intake became legendary, Waller and his close friend Earl Hines (arguably the greatest jazz pianist of the ages) were bested by two chorus girls. Hines and Fats were relaxing in Waller's dressing room between shows, and Fats proudly displayed a new bottle which he intended to share with his "jug buddy." Enter the two chorines, who cooed and giggled and asked if they might have a teeny sip. Waller obliged and was about to partake seriously when the next show was announced. He and Hines left. When they returned, the cuties were gone and the bottle stood empty.

"Good God," Waller said. "Those girls are spoilin' my reputation!"

Waller arranged to drink during stage shows by having a valet standing in the wings, holding a tray with glasses, ice, soda water, and bottles of amber and silver joy. Waller would finish a number and announce to the audience, "Folks, it's time for a little libation," exit, quaff, sigh contentedly, return to the piano, and dive into the next number.

Fats enjoyed gargantuan meals of hearty fare, often ordering two or even three steaks at a time (once a waitress refused to bring the meal until "the other two in your party show up"). But he also had some notable encounters with hamburgers. In the mid-twenties, before he became successful as a composer, Waller was often on his uppers. Running into Fletcher Henderson, a popular and respected black orchestra leader (he later wrote arrangements that made Benny Goodman famous), Waller cajoled him into a meal. Henderson and his band members watched in awe as Fats consumed nine hamburgers and then offered to write nine songs for Henderson to work off his debt.

Several years later, while Fats was playing the Howard Theatre in Washington, D. C., during a furiously hot summer, Hines and other pals were in his dressing room when the door opened and ten burgers were brought in with an equal number of beers. Waller leaned forward eagerly, brushing away the extended hand of a guest: "Now, now, that's mine! If you want some, I'll be glad to order more, but this here belongs to me!"

Waller's talents and charm brought him an almost immediate national audience by 1934, when Fats had a weekly radio program over the CBS network and his small recording band, Fats Waller & His Rhythm, began making the first of many hits for RCA Victor. Waller's national tours were drawing hundreds of thousands to clubs, and he was soon to make his first movie appearances.

His radio stardom provided some creepy moments for executives. Broadcasting from a nightclub where he was politely applauded after each number (the big crowd hadn't come in yet), he yelled into the radio mike: "Don't be fooled, folks, there's nobody here but me and the waiters." And CBS was too slow to bleep him when he concluded a show with: "I'd like to close with a message to my dear wife—get that man outta there, honey, 'cause I'm comin' home directly!"

Waller the personality eventually overpowered Waller the musician in the public eye. But he was one of the best jazz pianists who ever lived. "Stride" piano of the type that Waller played is often mistaken for the ragtime from which it came, or for the boogie-woogie style that took the most obvious features of stride and simplified them to the point of monotony. Wherever he was booked, Waller insisted that the contract provide for a Steinway grand, freshly tuned, and that he not be obliged to play boogie. It bored him.

Most pianists are one-handed, depending on the right hand for everything while the left chords on the bass and baritone keys. But stride, perfected by James P. Johnson (who wrote *Charleston* and *If I Could Be with You One Hour Tonight*), brought a new role to the left hand. No longer would it just keep the beat; it would have equal power and responsibilities. Treble, bass, baritone, and soprano keys would all work together. More, the left hand could suspend the rhythm, keep it dangling, and build up suspense—then suddenly bring the rhythm back for drama and color.

At the turn of the century, when ragtime was at its peak, a group of Harlem pianists were playing in a style that would become the basis for stride. Some of them, such as The Shadow (no relation to Lamont Cranston) and Abba Labba, didn't have names; others are long forgotten: Freddy Bryant, Jess Pickett, and Jack the Bear. Directly after them came the pianists who polished and augmented the style: Charles Luckyeth Roberts, Eubie Blake, Willie Gant, Willie "The Lion" Smith, and Johnson. The last two evolved as the best performers of the style, with Johnson shading Smith. By the time Johnson taught and touted Waller, the three of them had formed an unbeatable triumvirate.

The greatness of stride was that it did not compromise the songs played for the sake of the style. Ragtime and boogie-woogie were locked into themselves and forced material to fit in their molds. Stride was open, free, generous, flexible. It could be barrelhouse or sophisticated, violent or tender. As such, it was perfectly suited to Waller's personality. He could swing like mad when he wanted to—and he often wanted to—but he took full advantage of the lyrical possibilities of stride. He had a touch of class that left a lasting impression.

Waller was a master of music and life. He loved both. He was exuberant, confident, and yea-saying. The last thing he would have anyone think of was death. Therefore, it may be best to get the matter of his leaving out of the way. Waller had no time for bad news, even his own.

He died at thirty-nine, but he looked nearly fifty. A musician's life and his appetites had taken their toll, but he had enormous energy and had always thrown off physical cares before.

After concluding a six-week run at the Florentine Gardens in Hollywood, Waller boarded a cross-country train with his manager, W.T. (Ed) Kirkeby, to get back to New York in time to spend Christmas with his family. It was December 15, 1943. In addition to his commercial bookings, Fats had gone out of his way to entertain troops at army bases and hospitals and he was very tired. He had only recently recovered from a serious attack of influenza, and his doctor had warned him that if he kept up his drinking habits they could be terminal. During his run at the Gardens, Waller had been placed on the bandstand near an air conditioner and had caught a chill. As the train pulled away and they found their compartment, Waller said to Kirkeby, in a rare complaint, "Oh, man, I can't take much more of this."

Waller was recognized on the train and invited to join a party, but he begged off to retire. Fats slept long hours when he did sleep so Kirkeby was not surprised at his absence and didn't worry about time. But when the train approached Kansas City, the weather turned bitterly cold. Coming into the compartment, Kirkeby was stunned by the rush of freezing air. "Yeah," Waller said, commenting on the lungs of his friend, saxophonist Coleman Hawkins, "Hawkins is really out there tonight."

Kirkeby retired, but at about four in the morning he awoke to see Waller's huge body shivering. There was a terrible choking sound, one final spasm, and Fats lay still. Kirkeby went running for a porter, demanding a doctor. The train pulled into the station—the same station where, nine years before, Pretty Boy Floyd and his cohorts had bungled a rescue attempt for safecracker Frank "Jelly" Nash by mowing down Nash and his escort of unarmed FBI agents.

The frantic Kirkeby located a doctor who briefly examined Waller and said, "This man is dead." A porter heard the news; it spread through the station and onto another train headed west. On that train was Louis Armstrong. Hearing of Waller's death, he burst into tears and cried all night.

The diagnosis was bronchial pneumonia, a sudden and vicious attack.

Earl Hines remembered:

> Fats and I had been out in California, and we were sitting in a garden. We were talking, and he said he was going back to New York. So was I in a few days, so we made a date to meet. The next day some guy comes up to me and says, "Did you hear about Fats?" And I said no, and he said, "He's dead." I looked at the guy, and I thought he must be high on something. I said, "That can't be; I was with him yesterday." Now there's a story—I don't know whether it's true or not—that when he was found there was a case of Scotch in the room and he had a bottle in his hand. I don't know whether the whiskey got there because someone thought they would give him a present or whether it was someone who knew his situation—Fats was laying off the stuff on doctor's orders—and had it in for him. Because there're a lot of jealous people around, you know, and maybe someone wanted to do him wrong. I tried to trace that to find out if it was true and who might have done it. I had people working on that for six months, but I was never able to find out.

Kirkeby, still in shock, brought the body to New York. Services were held at the Abyssinian Baptist Church in Harlem, where Waller's family had often worshiped. The pastor was the young Reverend Adam Clayton Powell; it would be some years before Powell became a congressman and pursued his parallel career of buffoonery and debauch. Powell's wife at the time was Hazel Scott, a superior jazz pianist and singer who worked the more intimate clubs in Harlem and downtown "Swing Street," on Fifty-second, off Sixth Avenue. She had a style of phrasing that was closely studied by young Frank Sinatra.

Hazel Scott played *Abide with Me* on the organ. It had been Waller's and his mother's favorite melody. Four thousand people jammed into the church and an adjoining settlement house or stood in the street or on the rooftops to hear the services broadcast over loudspeaker. Born and raised in Harlem, Waller was a community hero.

The coffin and the sides of the pulpit were banked with so many flowers that they formed a rectangle nine feet high and twenty feet wide. Powell mounted to the pulpit and began: "Fats Waller's sweetest songs are yet to be heard, in Heaven." He recalled the days when he and Waller were playmates (other neighborhood kids were Edgar Sampson, who wrote *Stompin' at the Savoy,* and the great black actor Canada Lee). Looking at the crowd, Powell rose to new heights of banality, saying: "Fats Waller always played to a packed house."

Gene Buck, ex-president of ASCAP (which had recognized Waller as a composer once he became nationally popular[1]) who had rounded up ASCAP members as honorary pallbearers, eulogized Waller as bringing "great distinction to his family, his race, nation, colleagues, and friends."

The service concluded, Waller's coffin was borne into the street, where several women stepped from the crowd to take flowers from the casket as a remembrance. Winter sunshine touched the tenements. Onlookers in the street and on the roofs later swore that a

---

[1]ASCAP at this time was also uninterested in country and western music. Singing cowboy Gene Autry testified before Congress that his application for membership had twice been rejected until he became a major box office movie attraction, after which he was accepted with alacrity.

special ray of sunlight struck and spilled over the casket, which was loaded into the hearse and driven to Maspeth, Long Island, where the body was cremated. It was December 20, 1943.

Downtown, at the Broadhurst Theatre on Broadway, *Early to Bed,* for which Waller had written the music, was playing to good business; producer Richard Kollmar had been negotiating with Waller for a second show. *Stormy Weather* was a successful film. Waller's records were still selling, and the many transcription performances he had made on "V-discs" for the troops were being broadcast to European and Pacific foxholes.

It was strange and sudden to have him gone; surely he might have said to death, as he said in *The Joint is Jumpin':* "No, baby, not now; I can't come over there right now."

But here we are done with death. Let us move on to a remarkable life.

2
Stayin' at Home

HARLEM DID NOT EXIST as a black community when Edward Martin Waller and his wife Adeline Lockett arrived in New York. Most of the black population of the city was confined to an area of Greenwich Village known as "South Fifth Avenue."

Around the turn of the century "South Fifth Avenue" underwent one of the many migratory recomplexions common to New York. Irish and Italian families displaced the blacks, who moved farther up the West Side to the Sixties. The blacks' new locale was known either as "The Jungles" or as "San Juan Hill."

While The Jungles was a black nickname for the new tough area, the alternate title had a great deal to do with black pride. It commemorated the exploits of the black Twenty-fourth and Twenty-fifth Infantry and Ninth and Tenth Cavalry, which had one of the most distinguished service records in the Spanish-American War of 1898. Although Colonel Theodore Roosevelt's volunteer corps of college boys and cowhands, known as the Rough Riders, came away with the publicity, it is doubtful whether they would have survived the war without the efforts of the black troops. The Rough Riders were long on dash and bravado but short on military experience. The black units were composed of "career privates."

At Las Guisamas the Rough Riders were pinned down by a crossfire of well-emplaced Spanish rifles and cannon. Annihilation of the giddy amateurs was a likely possibility until the professional black troopers, singing *There'll Be a Hot Time in the Old Town Tonight,* pounced on the Spanish positions in a series of hand-to-hand combats, broke up the crossfire, and allowed Roosevelt's lads to advance. Not long afterward, they helped clear the way at San Juan Hill, practically making a gift of the crest to the Rough Riders. To Roosevelt's credit—and to that of his unit—the Rough Riders always acknowledged the part the black troops had played. Roosevelt was fond of quoting the opinion of the Rough Riders after the battle: "Well, those Ninth and Tenth men are all right. They can drink out of our canteens." In an era when drinking fountains were segregated, this was no small praise.

But whether known as San Juan Hill or The Jungles, the West Side area was unsatisfying to middle-class blacks or to blacks with middle-class hopes. The section bordered on the ferocious Hell's Kitchen neighborhood, which had replaced the old Five Points of the Bowery as the dwelling place of the Irish street gangs. By 1900 a substantial number of Italian families had entered Hell's Kitchen, and soon after that the first blacks moved in, as space in The Jungles was used up. Thus there were three-cornered hostilities. The power of the gangs gradually decreased, but the absence of battle—poverty's merrymaking—served only to call more attention to overcrowding and social stagnation. Respectable blacks with labor skills or a talent for commerce longed for a place of peace, quiet, and room.

At the same time that South Fifth Avenue was changing ethnically, a group of real estate speculators commissioned the brilliant architect and chronic womanizer Stanford White to design a block of luxury houses and apartments in the undeveloped Harlem. White[2] completed the assignment in 1901, and construc-

---

[2]On a summer night in 1906, White was shot dead on the rooftop of Madison Gardens by Harry Dexter Thaw, rich and neurotic husband of former Ziegfeld Follies showgirl Evelyn Nesbitt. The lady claimed that White had compromised her honor before her marriage. One of her other premarital suitors was the gifted and handsome actor John Barrymore, who dropped a rose petal into a glass of milk and told her, "That is your mouth."

tion began. Located on 139th Street between Seventh and Eighth avenues, the project was handsome, expensive, and an immediate failure. Built to lure wealthy whites, it was too far "north" at a time when Fifty-seventh Street was considered to be the "top of the town" for business, residence, and pleasure; when stage theaters had only lately been a-building in Times Square (several major theaters were in the Thirty-fourth Street area); when the subway system was still primitive and limited. Harlem was too inconvenient for persons who liked to consider themselves at the center of things.

Stanford White's buildings went untenanted until a black real estate agent, E. Phillip Payton—surely he deserves to be called "The Father of Harlem"—persuaded the white developers to rent to wealthy and middle-class black families. The houses were converted into apartments, and the first of the new arrivals, delighted to breathe the fresh air and contemplate the treelined streets, moved in. White's original block later came to be known as "Striver's Row," and sometimes as "Sugar Hill"—"sugar" being black slang for "money."

As more families moved northward to Harlem (the district was named by the original Dutch settlers in the 1600s after the city of Haarlem, a seaport in the Netherlands), additional dwellings between 130th and 140th streets and between Fifth and Seventh avenues were converted, larger apartments being broken into cubbyholes and "closet parlors." But as late as 1918 the now famous thoroughfare of 125th Street was still exclusively white.

Until the United States entered World War I in 1917, the black population of New York was limited and largely city-born for several generations. The upper strata of the black community were as careful of their public and private behavior as were their white counterparts. Social behavior was very much of a nineteenth-century cast—polite, aloof, and slightly stuffy.

This "old morality" took a serious whacking in 1917, when thousands of blacks from the rural South and the islands of the West Indies flocked to New York (as well as other northern cities) for work in war industries. Militarily unprepared as always, the United States had to feed, clothe, equip, shelter, train, and transport an army of millions at once. Enormous vacancies for unskilled labor were quickly filled by the arriving blacks, who jammed into the available housing in Harlem and caused even more territory to be made available to them.

Though the war boom of jobs vanished after 1918, most of the new Harlemites elected to stay; underpaid by national standards, they still earned a better living in the North than they could possibly hope to earn in the nonindustrialized South, and in Harlem they had much greater social freedom because of their concentration in a large cohesive community.

The diversity and creativity of Harlem's people reached a peak in the 1920s and 1930s which has never been, and probably never will be, equaled. Both the social and the artistic culture were genuine and instinctive. The mixture of city-born sophisticates, farm innocents, and island sprites was bewildering and fascinating. Harlem was an outlandish tangle of brilliance, ambition, balderdash, and sloth. Literary activity—"the Harlem Renaissance"—brought attention to the poets James Weldon Johnson, Countee Cullen, and Langston Hughes, and the novelist Claude McKay. But these were highfalutin matters. Harlem's great talent was to be sensual, and its sensuality was expressed as entertainment in theater, dance, and music, and in the splendor and braggadocio of individual personality. On arriving in Harlem from sedate Washington, D. C., in 1923, the young pianist, composer, and bandleader Duke Ellington exclaimed: "Why, it is just like the Arabian Nights!"

One of the talents and personalities already making it that way was Thomas Wright Waller.

Edward Martin Waller, Thomas' father, was born about 1870 in Bermuda Hundred, Virginia, scene of an amphibious Civil War battle. In the late 1880s he married Adeline Lockett, who is said to have been attractive and possessed of a good singing voice and skill at the piano and organ. Shortly after their marriage, Edward Martin Waller announced that he had no intention of raising children in the South. He went to New York, found work in a stable, saved his money, returned to Virginia, and departed again for the city with his wife after a gala farewell given by his friends. The Wallers settled on South Fifth Avenue's Waverly Place around 1889. Their first child was born the following year, one of seven to die as a consequence of the high infant mortality rates of the time.

Thomas Wright Waller was born on May 21, 1904, when the family had settled on 134th Street, one block away from what was to become the *camino real* of Harlem. In the intervening years, when the family lived on West Sixty-third Street in The Jungles, Waller's brothers Robert and Edward were born. The last children were his sisters Naomi and Edith. By 1910 the fecund Adeline, always a large girl, had become corpulent and had contracted diabetes. Her illness and the energy required to look after five children brought an end to her conceiving.

Little is known of Waller's father except that he was thin, had cured himself of a boyhood stammer, was actively religious, and thoroughly disapproved of Thomas' jazz career.

Soon after they arrived at South Fifth Avenue, the Wallers joined the Abyssinian Baptist Church, then located at Fortieth Street (the present building was completed in 1923), and Edward Martin became a deacon while Adeline sang in the choir and played the piano and the organ for services. Thomas' exposure at infancy to the terrific wallop and poetic frenzy of black church music stayed with him through his life, as did his preference for the pipe organ. In the late 1930s Ashton Stevens, the Chicago drama and music critic, wrote: "The organ is the instrument of Waller's heart; the piano that of his stomach." Thomas' adulation of his mother probably also contributed to his respect for the pipe organ.

The Wallers' homelife featured a good deal of hymn singing, with Adeline providing accompaniment on the harmonium, a wheezy and nasal reed organ. It was this "poor man's calliope" that Waller first learned to play, around 1909, by which time he was also experimenting with an upstairs neighbor's piano.

In the following year Edward Martin, then chairman of the Board of Deacons and superintendent of the Sunday School of the Abyssinian Baptist Church, heard a Reverend Morris of the Pentecostal persuasion preach with sweat and fire. Edward Martin and Adeline thereupon got rebaptized at the Refuge Temple on 133d Street; their children dutifully followed suit. Pentecostal believers are either quietly and privately comfortable with the

true word—it is the egg they nest upon—or abrasive and nag-
ging about it to the unsaved, in which case they sling eggs at
passersby.

Edward Martin appears to have been the egg-slinging type; he
took up street preaching shortly after his rebaptism, with Adeline singing and young Thomas playing the harmonium. Tom's
reaction to his father's public harangues was most likely a mixture of embarrassment and pride—the latter for his mother's
sake, for Adeline was as devout as her husband.

Black Christianity, as practiced by the Baptist denomination,
which has always been the predominant force of the black reaction to the mighty tale of Jesus, has always been a source of
comfort and pride to blacks as well as something of a private
joke. Though black Christianity's record in living and acting on
the golden rule is equal to that of white Christianity, black
Christianity has suffered from being gullible to the many loud-
mouthed scalawags, demagogues, and hustlers with talents for
bamboozling who have historically bilked the faithful.

The spiritual swindlers in black churches owed some of their
success to the nearly automatic respect given to announced men
of the cloth in black communities, since blacks had so few other
public notables to applaud and follow. Until very recently,
blacks did not participate in the upward economic life of the
nation in general; nearly all their heroes were entertainers or
preachers.

The zanier antics of black divines, elders of the church, and
the sanctified "sisters"—the older females of the congregation
who are traditionally the most devoted to the church's affairs—
have more than once been the subject of gentle parody and lov-
ing contempt by black jazz artists. Louis Armstrong, Waller's
firm friend, recorded a hilarious and humiliating satire of a
country "camp meeting" in his 1931 version of the old spiritual
Lonesome Road, presenting himself as the "Reverend Satchel-
mouth" (a part he had played in vaudeville) taking up a collection:

I wanta thank yuh for this collection. Of cawse, it could'a been
bettuh—two mo' dollahs would'a got my shoes outta pawn. . . .

(High-pitched female scream in background) Hold that sistuh!
And git offa my foot! But nevertheless I'm in love witcha. . . .
And if yuh got anythin', bruthuh, please don't keep it in yo'
pocket. . . .

Young Tom's sisters recalled after his death that he played up
his part as his mother's favorite child by cagily bringing in religious devotion when it got him into something he wanted, such
as the cookie jar, or out of trouble. His chief ally in mischief—
and the one who always caught the punishment—was Waller's
sister Naomi. Tom was usually able to dodge justice by conning
his mother with tales of how he'd dreamed of the Gentle Shepherd.

The Waller children were generally kept indoors as much as
possible, since their parents thought association with other children on the street might corrupt them. But Adeline's failing
health and Edward Martin's long working hours—he had started
in the nineties as a stableman and had gone on to build up his
own cartage business—gave the Waller brood more freedom. On
one occasion Adeline's Christian charity took her out of the
house while she cared for a neighbor's child who was seriously
ill. The other Waller sons and daughters were more grown up
and spending more time out of the house. So a lonely Thomas,
feeling neglected, began to sample the considerable Harlem
nightlife, skipped school, and made his parents frantic. A few
days later he showed up at the house of a friend and told his
pal's folks that he had run away from home because his father
had thrown him out. Tom was sent home the next day and
given a cold-eyed dressing down by Edward Martin, who announced a thrashing as punishment. Tom first tried to outstep
his father, then raised a fist in defiance, but he was quickly made
to feel the belt strap. Adeline watched in anguish and fell sick.
Tom had been humiliated, and he cannot have felt kindly toward Edward Martin for causing (as Tom saw it) a relapse in his
mother's condition, nor could he have been much in sympathy
with his father's complaint that the doctor's visit cost $10.

But most of the incidents in Tom's childhood were pleasant.
There was a close family relationship and a sense of security

which many black children—then or now—do not feel. Whatever his failings, Edward Martin was a definite and consistent father figure as well as a good provider. There was always food on the table (pianist Charles Luckyeth Roberts remembered that the family "pushed a mean crumb")—so much so that Thomas had picked up the nickname "Fats" before he reached puberty. He was then attending Public School 89, located next to the Waller apartment building, so that Adeline could lean out of her window and yell into the windows of the school, "How's Tom doin'?"

Tom was doing all right but was not an outstanding student, except in the school orchestra, where he played violin and piano, mugged and joked for his classmates, and followed the baton of student conductor Edgar Sampson, who later wrote and arranged *Stompin' at the Savoy*. Another of Waller's classmates was the great black actor Canada Lee, who played in the Broadway production of Richard Wright's bitter *Native Son* in 1941, and later in the decade as Macbeth in an all-black presentation; both plays were directed by the young genius Orson Welles.

The best moment in Tom's young life was the day in 1910 when he was sent out on a long errand and returned to find a Waters upright piano in the living room. Though piano lessons were theoretically intended for Naomi (as a skill that every young girl of good family should possess), Tom was the acknowledged prodigy. Naomi and Tom were to be taught by a Miss Perry. Neither Waller child was interested in theory or in learning things by rote, but Tom, using his already considerably developed charm, persuaded his instructor to play a popular song twice. A few days later at home, working the Waters upright, he was playing the piece confidently, depending on his remarkable ear and his visual memory of the way Miss Perry's fingers walked over the keys.[3]

By 1915 Tom's musical talents were so evident that Edward Martin, who denounced his son's ragtime interpolations into the

---

[3]While Waller was using his infant ear, another child piano prodigy, white Bix Beiderbecke, was doing the same thing in Davenport, Iowa. These two "modern" pianists will be compared in a later chapter.

playing of hymns as "the Devil's music" but admired his skill, gave up on his idea of seeing Tom enter the church as a minister. At the same time, he hoped to lure his son away from mere popular music by exposing him to classical fare. He therefore took him to hear an Ignace Paderewski recital at Carnegie Hall.[4] Thomas was enormously impressed by the Pole's technique as well as by the European ideas of composition and harmony. It was an instinctive reaction on Tom's part; all his life he was able to store basic knowledge and convert it into polished art at great speed, after mastering the mechanics of the musical forms he wished to work in. It is easy to imagine the eleven-year-old Waller's awe and delight at Carnegie Hall that evening. It may not be too much to imagine that among the few other black persons in attendance was the ragtime king Scott Joplin, already half-mad with syphilis and frustration over the rejection of his opera *Treemonisha*. Joplin's artistic, ambitious vision was to fuse Negro rhythms he learned in his youth while playing in mining camps, oil towns, bars, and whorehouses with classical European harmonic ideas, and to dominate both with his superb talent for melody. Thomas Waller's ideas were roughly similar. Joplin would die on April Fools' Day, 1917.

But whatever healthy influence Edward Martin hoped the Paderewski concert would have on his youngest and most mercurial son, he could not prevent Fats from hearing and being impressed by the popular music of the time, nor could he hope to keep him sheltered from the way the world was carrying on.

---

[4]Paderewski became the first president of Poland after the nation again gained independence in 1920. In the early 1930s, he appeared in a Hollywood film, *Moonlight Sonata,* titled after Beethoven's piece, which the pianist had made his signature and cursed trademark. He was more the celebrity than the star of the picture. Invited as a houseguest by a wealthy family, he prevents the pretty ninny daughter from breaking off her engagement with a nice fellow by advising her to lure her swain into the garden while he steps through the French doors to the music room. Hedging his bets, Paderewski says: "Perhobbs da 'Moon-lide Zhonada' wull wark idzh modgyck wance aw-gehn." The magic works again; the lovers are reunited as Paderewski plays, wiggling his snowy luxurious eyebrows in the manner of God. I give this synopsis because it is not substantially different from the roles Waller played in films.

3
Lost Love

TOM'S EARLY EXPLORATIONS into Harlem nightlife (still wearing short pants, he would not have been allowed inside the clubs) acquainted him with the styles of many pianists. Nearly all of them were playing theatrical accompaniments to singers whose material, style, and delivery were based on the many black touring shows. These shows were revues with slapstick comedy and musical interludes; they were not in any sense the whole creations that the typical American musical comedy is today.

Quite likely, one of Tom's boyhood friends who had a phonograph played him the recordings of Bert Williams, the brilliant black entertainer described by W. C. Fields as "the funniest man I ever saw and the saddest man I ever knew." Initially teamed with the gifted George Walker (who, like Joplin, died of syphilis, a not uncommon disease among blacks and whites, for which there was then no cure), Williams starred in such cheap and desperate productions as *Bandana Land, In Dahomey* and *Under the Ham Tree,* shabby entertainments predicated on a picture of the black as being lazy, wily, greedy, stupid, and frightened. But Williams' artistry was so powerful and his appeal

so great that from 1905 until his death in 1922 (the year Fats
first recorded) he starred in the most fabulous and legendary of
Broadway revues, *The Ziegfeld Follies,* playing with W. C. Fields
and Eddie Cantor.

Williams' most endearing and lasting routine began with his
white-gloved hands flapping between closed curtains while the
pit band struck up the opening notes of his hallmark song, *Nobody,* which he recorded between 1909 and 1911, and again in
1915, the year Tom went to see Paderewski. Williams' lyrics are
worth reproducing, since they say in essence the same thing as
Waller's *Black and Blue* (with lyrics by Andy Razaf). Both were
statements of black facts of living disguised as entertainment:

> When summer comes all cool and clear
> And friends they see me coming near
> Who says, "Come in and have a beer"?
>
> Nobody!
>
> I ain't never done nothin' to nobody
> I ain't never got nothin' from nobody, no time;
> And until I get somethin' from somebody sometime
> I don't intend to do nothin' for nobody, no time.

Tom would also have been familiar with the name of James
Reese Europe, the tall and handsome orchestra leader and
founder in 1910 of the Clef Club, which was meant to be both a
fraternity for "legitimate" (formally trained) black musicians and
a booking office for orchestral engagements at the many fine
hotels and supper clubs in New York.

Reese obtained a commission as a major when the United
States entered World War I in 1917. His mission was to form a
military band to complement and cheer on the thousands of
black troops, many of whom were volunteers. He succeeded
most admirably; his band participated in many victory parades
in France and at home. Tom must have been shocked to learn,
in 1919, that Europe had been stabbed to death by a lunatic
drummer in his orchestra.

The war produced other Harlem heroes. One, Private Henry
Johnson, would have had a special meaning, since he was att-

ached to the glorious 369th regiment, an all-black unit whose ranks included Tom's brother Lawrence Robert (he had put up the money for the Waters upright piano). The 369th was the first American combat unit to see action and, like its black predecessors in the Spanish-American fracas, may have had the most distinguished fighting record of the 1918 war. Lawrence Robert Waller was listed as missing in action (mother Adeline wept with anxiety and father Edward Martin, predictably, depended on God's will), but he was eventually found safe. When he returned home in the Harlem victory parade led by James Reese Europe's band, Lawrence Robert Waller might well have told the story of "The Battle of Henry Johnson."

When the United States became a combatant in 1917, both the Allied Powers and the Central Powers had exhausted much of their manpower as well as the scant imaginations of their generals. The Allied General Staff was dominated by the French, who that year had secretly put down a mutiny in their army (the cynical *poilus* marched to the front baaing like sheep at their commanders), and who now demanded that fresh American troops, fully trained or not, be placed in combat immediately.

General John J. "Black Jack" Pershing, thus nicknamed because he had once commanded Negro units, was forced to assign troops to a particularly sensitive sector on the Franco-Belgian border. He chose the 369th,[5] who were issued French helmets

---

[5]Contemporary demagogues have falsely charged that the combat use of black troops is and has been "racist," i. e., that black soldiers are considered "expendable" because of their color. However, Pershing's decision to use the 369th was based on his professional evaluation and experience of the discipline, cohesiveness, and fighting qualities of Negro troops. The French had the same appreciation of their colonial Senegalese units.

In 1917 the federal government foolishly sent black units to be trained in such hostile southern towns as Spartanburg, South Carolina, where Sergeant Noble Sissle (who collaborated with Eubie Blake to write the first great black musical, *Shuffle Along*) was cursed and beaten by a hotel owner when Sissle tried to buy a newspaper in the lobby. Forty white soldiers jumped the owner and were about to demolish him and his hotel when they were smartly called to attention by a bellow from Lieutenant James Reese Europe, who ordered them to leave the lobby in columns of twos. The soldiers obeyed their superior officer.

and the Gallic three-shot Lebel rifle and placed under French command.

It was night on the battlefield. Private Henry Johnson was crouched in a filthy trench where the lice held court. He was on guard against probing German patrols. American prisoners were a premium item to the Kaiser's army, for German intelligence officers were extremely eager to learn of Yankee training, equipment, and attitudes toward the war. They soon found out through Johnson.

A surprise attack killed or wounded most of Johnson's trench buddies, and he himself was shot through the lower abdomen, close to the bowels. Yet when the Germans jumped into the trench, the desperately wounded Johnson popped off three of them with his Lebel rifle clip, clubbed another with the butt of his gun, and chased a party who were trying to carry off his wounded friend, Private Needham Roberts. Johnson took his razor-sharp bayonet and disposed of the kidnappers. The clubbed German said, in perfect English, "The little black son of a bitch has got me," and Johnson yelled back: "Yes, he has, and if you don't look out, this little black son of a bitch is gonna get you again!" The German made a move, and Johnson, with his bayonet, opened him up from the stomach to the chin. Then, still with his awful wound, Johnson hurled grenades at the retreating Germans, who were not prepared for such superb warring from a man who had been an underpaid baggage clerk at the railroad station in Albany, New York.

The French showered decorations on Johnson and, recovered from his wounds, he marched proudly in the victory parade in Paris. When the parade was repeated in Harlem in 1919—with Lawrence Robert Waller among the troops—it must have been an ecstatic fifteen-year-old Thomas who cheered from his seat on the curb.

Waller had already left school the year before. He and his sister Naomi held jobs briefly in a jewel box factory in the Battery; Fats used his lunch hours to ingratiate himself with a sexton of the famous Trinity Church so that he could practice on its piano. One of his sessions brought him back to work late; the boss rode him over the coals, and Fats, who didn't need much of an excuse, used the incident as an excuse to quit.

He'd also been doing some ingratiating at the Lincoln movie and vaudeville theater on 135th Street, near the Waller home. The house pianist was a Mazie Mullins, who was soon letting the teenager sit in while she took a break. Waller was also casting eyes at the theater pipe organ. The white owner, Marie Downes, agreed with pianist Mullins that the balloon-shaped boy was precocious on both instruments, if a trifle hesitant on technique. But, as always, Waller learned with amazing speed. When the regular organist suddenly became ill, Waller deputized for him, and when Mazie Mullins left, Marie Downes offered Waller the position as house keyboardist at a salary of $23 a week—big money in 1919.

Edward Martin and Adeline were woeful and slightly wrathful when they heard of Thomas' engagement, since any building other than a church or their home was, of course, a sink of sin. But it had become so apparent that Thomas' future lay with music that his parents, not for the first time, sighed and resigned themselves.

They would have been even more concerned to know that Thomas was beginning to make the acquaintance of jazz musicians. Saturday nights at the Lincoln featured vaudeville attractions as well as small orchestras. It is highly probable that Waller saw Bert Williams perform at the Lincoln. Among the other notables in the Saturday night crowds were orchestra leaders, theatrical booking agents, and talent scouts. Amiable since birth, Waller made friends quickly and began to keep the late hours which were later to be part of his legend. No doubt he also drank his first liquor; the jazz and theatrical brotherhoods are historically boozy. Whatever his first drink tasted like, it probably went down sweeter for the adventure and the approaching danger of lawbreaking, for national Prohibition was due to become law in 1920.

Around this time Waller played his first band engagement as a pianist at a dance on 165th Street and Brook Avenue. He met a girl named Edith Hatchett and several days later brought her home for dinner. The family was surprised at Fats' boldness, for he had seldom seemed interested in girls. Edith was well-

mannered and soft-spoken, which counted, and actively religious, which immediately made her acceptable to Adeline and
Edward Martin. She became a frequent dinner guest.

Waller's interest in jazz—he could not play it in 1920—
increased, and although the ragtime era had ended in 1917 with
the death of Scott Joplin, half a dozen Harlem pianists were
beginning to develop their own style of music, with highly individual ideas and techniques. The style became known as "stride,"
and James P. Johnson was already its master and dean. Waller
sought an introduction to him, and so went to see Russell
Brooks, older brother of a school friend and a local keyboard
hero. Fats found Brooks playing a dance date in a tent-covered
vacant lot at 140th Street and Lenox Avenue. Brooks agreed to
set up a meeting, and the overjoyed Fats, lost in dreams and
probably imagining his first handshake with Johnson, managed
to get his legs tangled in the ropes that held up the tent and to
pull the whole canvas down. It was not the last time Waller
made a crowd roar.

But the summer of 1920 was to be the most terrible of
Waller's life. His adored Adeline, though suffering from diabetes
and depleted in strength from her childbearing and her home
duties, had grown monstrously fat. Her bulk put great pressure
on her circulatory system and heart and, like most diabetics, she
was always tempted to eat prohibited items. She was not yet
fifty years old when she crashed to the floor, dead.

The shock and horror of his mother's death were cruelly complicated by the humiliating removal of her body. Too big to get
through the front door of the apartment building and over the
stoop on which Waller, years before, had painted the family
name, her corpse was taken out through a window by a block
and tackle. Whether Waller saw the ghastly procedure is not
known, but the thought of it must have continually chilled him.

While Edward Martin mumbled orthodox sentiments about
the Lord's talent for taking away, Fats went into shock. His
older brothers and sisters were married; he, Naomi, and his father were left. Waller found it too painful to walk through his
own door. Wilson Brooks, his school pal, came home to find
Fats sitting on the Brooks doorstep with a face that seemed

ready to slide into his lap. Waller told Wilson that he couldn't and wouldn't go back to his own house. Wilson Brooks took Fats inside and put him to sleep on the sofa. The next morning a family conference decided that Fats' stay with the Brookses should be open-ended. Edward Martin gave his approval; he was dividing his time between living with his married children and maintaining residence at his own home. There was nothing he or his son could do for each other. Edward Martin did, however, have a use for unmarried Naomi, who acted as his housekeeper.

Waller's stay at the Brookses was happy and productive. Armed with a bowl of cut fruit and a loaf of bread, he studied the player piano the Brookses owned, feeding it piano rolls made by James P. Johnson. Waller would stop the action, spread his fingers over the depressed keys, and try to emulate the maestro's handspan. Waller worked particularly hard on Johnson's classic *Carolina Shout*. He very much wanted Johnson to be his mentor and was counting on Russell Brooks to arrange the meeting. One day Russell arrived for a visit to the family and watched Waller practicing. Remembering his promise, he spoke to Johnson a few days later, and James P. agreed to an interview.

An extraordinarily polite and patient man, James P. was also an extremely busy one, on constant call from Harlem·clubs, vaudeville agencies, and music publishers as pianist, accompanist, and tunesmith. Most likely, he agreed to see Waller because Brooks had pushed hard on the theme that young Tom was talented and in awe of him. Johnson, could not have been displeased.

Johnson's wife, Lillian May, recalled that he first went to the Lincoln Theatre to hear Waller play organ, then came home and told her, "I know I can teach that boy."

He could, and he did. Their master-pupil friendship resulted in the golden age of Harlem keyboarding.

4
Numb Fumblin'

IT IS NO WONDER that Tom Waller set out to woo James P. Johnson as his teacher and sponsor—in all things having to do with music, Waller usually showed good taste and a healthy ambition to advance himself.

In 1920, James P. Johnson was already the acknowledged master of what was known as the "stride" piano style, with some close competition from Willie "The Lion" Smith. In these days of limp piano playing, where the right hand picks out a simple melody while the left plays basic supporting rhythm chords, it may be difficult to conceive of a time when nearly all pianistics were firmly and ruggedly two-handed, from both compositional and performing standpoints.

"Stride," as it was developed by a half dozen innovators in The Jungles before World War I, kept the left hand as yeoman support but also provided it with greater rhythmic freedom. Instead of playing consistent full-bodied chords, the "stride" left hand played chords and single notes alternately. This gave an aggressive lift and bounce to the left hand that had not been heard in jazz piano before.

At first, the right hand played blues or ragtime variations. But

with the entrance of Johnson and Smith—who were fully acquainted and experienced with the theatrical and light-classical
modes of the early 1900s era, and familiar with Joplin's ideas of
combining European thematic sentiments with black rhythms—
the right hand also found greater areas to explore. Neither Johnson nor Smith were classically trained or knew much about
book-learning musical theory; whatever they did was done
mostly by ear and imagination. But their sentiments as composers were the same as those of Debussy, Liszt, or Chopin: airy,
introspective, humanistic, and tender. Combining these sentiments with the bubbly and potent rhythm of "stride" made for a
style that was an exciting, consistent contrast of the sweet and
the muscular.

In 1914 James P. Johnson wrote *Carolina Shout,* nominally a
ragtime piece but already destructive of the formal ragtime
preached by Joplin; the *Shout* was gay, bold, speedy, and sassy,
entirely without the melancholy that typified Joplin's work and
was thought to be mandatory for "serious" piano composition
among artistic ragtimers. Like Louis Armstrong, whose young
and volcanic solo talent destroyed the orthodox concept of ensemble playing in New Orleans jazz, Johnson's brilliance codi-
fied the new ideas about piano composition that his contempor-
aries had sensed and dreamed about.

Born in 1894 in New Brunswick, New Jersey, Johnson was
taught piano by his mother. At eight years of age he was hired
by a neighborhood woman to play for four hours on certain
afternoons, with the stipulation that he not look behind him or
turn around at any time; James P. guessed later that these odd
and stringent rules were to keep him from seeing the male clientele who visited the house.

He went to extraordinary lengths to train himself as a musician, playing with the lights out so that he would know the keyboard by "feel," and developing a soft but certain "touch" by
draping a bedsheet over the keys. His efforts to make himself
and his instrument one force bordered on the gently fanatic; he
would have agreed with the great folksinger and guitarist Leadbelly that his chosen instrument was "half my life, and my wife
is the other half."

In Johnson's early years, the piano was a fact of life in any home that could afford one, and in many that could not. It was a source of inspiration, entertainment, and status. The phonograph was an infant machine; radio was a decade away. Basic musical instruction was a part of every child's life in school or through private tutoring; sheet music sales were the prime source of income for music publishers; homes in which no member of the family learned how to play had the automatic player piano, which reproduced sounds via a perforated paper roll inserted into the machine's chest, much as a tape cartridge is slid into a "deck" today. As his reputation grew, James P. was given an offer to perform by the QRS piano roll company in Buffalo, New York (which still exists). During the early 1920s he was making a roll every other week at $50 a shot.

In the first twenty years of this century the piano—as an instrument or as furniture—was not only a prestige item in homes but the box of the gods in many of the watering holes of Manhattan. Distinguished "ticklers" had individual styles of dress and individual mannerisms—the way they dusted off the piano stool, flicked the tails of their jackets as they sat, and personalized their test chords. "Ticklers" (or "professors," as they were also known) were the wandering troubadours of the eastern seaboard in the black communities, as much concerned about the quality of the pianos they played as any medieval bard might be about the lutes he found in his tour of castles. Every pianist of note had a special "sign-in" chord he played, not only to test the condition of the instrument, but to announce his presence and proclaim his mystique. "Ticklers" were idolized then, much as rock 'n' roll musicians are now, especially by the women, who equated musical with sexual skill. To maintain the persona of visiting prince, all notable "ticklers" dressed sharp, spoke softly, and conducted themselves in a manner of born dignity and noblesse oblige. Outside preaching, there was no better game.

Ticklers had to be able not only to play the popular tunes of the day but to provide accompaniment to visiting singers or resident vocal entertainers in the saloons, as well as demonstrate their own showpieces. Nearly all the material they played was semitheatrical, meant for dramatic performance. The first seventeen years of this century saw the end of a genteel musical atmosphere in which most tunes were heavily sentimental; passion was forbidden, although it could be implied by individual performers. The general disguise of emotion in popular song was bewildered innocence or betrayed plighting of troths, as evidenced by such titles as *Those Wedding Bells Shall Not Ring Out!* or that period prayer to astrology, *Come Down, Come Down, My Evening Star.*

The composers of these sugared ditties were not much different from Stephen Foster in that they had a commanding sense of melody, a European outlook on composition, some technical training, and a hope that the reigning kings and queens of the day might pick their tune to perform. A "hit song" of that time had to spread by word of mouth from town to town and was entirely dependent on a stage performer singing it on tour.

Music for gentlefolk extended into the presentations offered by owners of saloons in The Jungles and early Harlem, so much so that both black and white establishments had to program selections from light opera on Sundays if they did not wish the police to come a-knocking. Ticklers, therefore, had to know their stuff; if they were not conversant with the acceptable music of the time they had to be able to fake it. Most of them were able, especially those with superior ears, such as Willie Smith and James P. Johnson.

But the leftover Victorian gentility of that era not only made black pianists skillful, it introduced them to ideas and ways and means of composition that they might otherwise not have paid attention to; and in James P. Johnson's case it presented him with a taunting goal of dignity to which his talent responded with quiet fury.

Johnson decided, sometime before 1920, that he would be a serious composer. His technique and ideas were already fully formed; he played with an innate and unmistakable majesty. By 1925 he met and bested the challenge of writing for the musical theater; after 1930 he devoted himself to symphonic works. But even in 1920, when he accepted Tom Waller as a student, Johnson was already playing as a composer, in a Chopinesque but distinctly American style.

Though he had taken formal lessons from a Mr. Gianini before 1910, Johnson was largely self-taught. Like Willie "The Lion" Smith, and later Waller, the stride pianists studied with "legitimate" teachers when they could afford to and had the time. In his autobiography, Smith recalled first meeting Johnson in the fall of 1914 while Smith was playing a club in Atlantic City. Johnson's wife, Lillian Mae, was a popular singer on the club and vaudeville circuit; Johnson was her second husband (and a great improvement over the first, a tickler and pimp who operated under the name of "The Tonsil"). Johnson was mild and retiring; he stayed out of the way when Smith and Lillian Mae got into a shouting match about what key Smith was to play in for her accompaniment. They resolved the contest amiably, and the men became close friends. "The Lion," who couldn't bear to see anyone he liked going without a nickname, dubbed Johnson "The Brute," as he was later to tag Waller "Filthy."

When Tom Waller became his pupil, Johnson outlined basic musical theory for him, had Tom play everything he knew, corrected his fingering, showed him tickler's tricks, and took the lad around with him to the various clubs where he played as soloist, bandmaster, or accompanist to Lillian Mae. It was fortunate that she and her husband kept the same hours and that both were used to the performer's way of life, for Waller often came home with them after a night's work and practiced on the master's piano until five in the morning, at which time Lillian would have to chase him out if she and James P. intended to get any sleep.

"You've got to have rhythm; Jimmie Johnson taught me that," Waller said many years later. Young Tom, as was customary, learned with remarkable speed, and even at this early time (on the evidence of his first recordings) he already was stamping his style with a whimsical gaiety that Johnson—who always played like a composer—seldom showed.

It is also probably a good hunch that Johnson's attentions to him and the older man's many kindnesses and sponsorship into the close and proud fraternity of superior pianists made Waller consider Johnson a surrogate father. Certainly Johnson's affection and respect for Waller were open and oft-proclaimed to his

peer musicians and friends: such public displays were beyond
Edward Martin Waller's capability as a person or pater.

About 1921 Johnson introduced Waller to the Lion. Always a
peppery personality, and with rigid rules about good taste,
Smith took umbrage at the innocent Waller's unpressed and
rumpled suit (he'd probably spent the night on Johnson's couch)
and took an attitude of *lese majeste* when Waller greeted him as
though he were an old friend. "Get that guy out of here," he
snapped to Johnson. "He looks filthy." Johnson calmed Smith
down momentarily, but Waller raised the Lion's hackles again
by repeated and confident requests that he be allowed to play
Carolina Shout. After more persuasion by Johnson, Smith let
Waller at the piano. One performance of the *Shout* later, the
ever-mercurial Smith changed his manner completely, saying:
"Watch out, Jimmy; he's got it." From then on, the trio became
the three wise men of Harlem hot piano.

One of the many avenues that Johnson opened to Waller was
the lucrative area of recordings. As mentioned, Johnson was already a steady-selling artist via the QRS piano rolls. He introduced Waller to the company and recommended that it use him.
And when the Lion walked out of Leroy's Cafe in a huff, Johnson and his wife trained Waller to replace him (part of Tom's
job was to accompany Lillian as she danced and sang).

But it was Clarence Williams of Chicago who brought Waller
into the phonograph studios for the first time. When Williams
moved to New York from Chicago in 1922, he had already written *Baby, Won't You Please Come Home?* and *Royal Garden
Blues*. The latter became a jazz standard of the 1920s, and the
former is still heard. Williams was a generalized specialist—he
maintained simultaneous careers as music publisher, pianist (of
the yeoman stripe), occasional vocalist, manager of his wife Eva
Taylor's singing career, pickup bandleader, songwriter, and recording date foreman. Among the copyrights he owned when he
arrived in New York were *I Wish I Could Shimmie like My
Sister Kate* (which Louis Armstrong may have partly written)
and *Gulf Coast Blues,* which Williams arranged to have Bessie
Smith record on her first date—as her accompanist, he was in a
convenient position to do so.

It is fair to say that the two most momentous events in 1920, at least in American history, were the enactment of the Prohibition Amendment to the Constitution in January and the release of *Crazy Blues,* sung by Mamie Smith, a black vaudevillian, in August. Properly speaking, *Crazy Blues* was not a blues. But it was the first recording by a black artist deliberately aimed at what had not before been thought of as a distinct and unplumbed market: the black audience. After *Crazy Blues* sold somewhere around 1,500,000 copies, nobody at Okeh Records needed any more convincing. The label devised the term *race records* for their product by black artists, and the boom was on. The pianist behind Mamie Smith on *Crazy Blues* was the Lion; it was one of the few records he made during the 1920s. Willie, who was earning a very comfortable living in clubs and on tour, was not impressed by the flat rates paid to recording musicians—the remuneration simply wasn't worth his time.

James P. Johnson, although successful as a piano-roll performer since the teens of the century, did not get on phonograph records until 1921,[6] barely a year ahead of Waller. Tom was the only one of the Harlem trio stride kings to realize the comparatively easy money to be made from recordings, and he disliked road touring, which Johnson and Smith were used to, so he came to depend on recording dates and on sales of his tunes to music publishers for his living.

But all this was a few years ahead of him. In 1922 he nearly aborted his recording career by failing to show up for his first recording date. Fats had been handpicked by Clarence Williams, who was less than pleased by Tom's vanishing act. But it was impossible to stay mad at Waller, so when another Martin date came up in the fall of that year Fats was again chosen. This time he appeared, providing accompaniment to Sara Martin as she sang *'Tain't Nobody's Business if I Do,* which included the passage:

> If I holler for a copper
> When I'm beat up by my poppa
> 'Tain't nobody's business if I do . . .

---

[6]Johnson recorded several piano solos for Columbia Records in 1916, but the label did not release them—nor has it ever.

Waller's reputation as a pianist was so well established in Harlem at the time that when Ralph Peer, owner of the Southern Music Publishing Co. and a talent scout for Okeh, was casting a pianist for a solo record of a Southern copyright called *Muscle Shoals Blues,* he was persuaded to hire Waller. Eighteen years old, young Tom showed the effects of his training by Johnson: rock-steady rhythm and a crispness of performance. *Muscle Shoals Blues* and the flip side, *Birmingham Blues,* also show a cautious Waller; occasionally there are flashes of his pixie personality, but there is no showy display of technique or any conscious effort to entertain. Waller didn't take any chances on offending or frightening the recording director with surprises on his first record.[7] These two sides are practically the only examples of Waller keeping his temperament under strict control.

It was also apparent that Waller had failed to keep his temperament under control when he married his girl friend, Edith Hatchett, almost immediately after his mother's death. The couple moved in with Edith's parents, and a son, Thomas, Jr., was born not long afterward. Opinion is unanimous that Waller's marriage was a direct reaction to his mother's death. Had Waller postponed matrimony and diverted the energy of his grief entirely to music, he would have been spared the constant ducking and dodging of process servers who sought to slip him legal papers ordering his appearance in court to answer charges of failure to pay alimony and child support.

As Waller became successful in music, he realized his mistake in marrying young for the wrong reasons but he could never believe himself liable to pay for this mistake. His refusal to face life led him into some looney scrapes, which at one point threatened to jeopardize his career, and engendered in him an uncharacteristic bitterness. But all that was some years away.

---

[7]Although some discographies give *Muscle Shoals* as Waller's first studio performance, both the solo date and the accompaniment to Sara Martin werre made at about the same time. Mike Lipskin, stride pianist, Johnson/Waller scholar, and one of the last pupils of Willie "The Lion" Smith, reports that Waller gave the saxophonist in his combo, Eugene "Honeybear" Sedric, a gift copy of *'Tain't Nobody's Business if I Do* in the 1930s, describing it to Sedric as the first record he ever made.

5
Goin' About

WILLIE THE LION gave a perturbed look over his shoulder. He turned from the bar where he, Tom, and James P. were drinking pre-Prohibition liquor and stalked across the room, edging his way through the guests gathered at the Park Avenue soiree, until he came to the thin-faced young man with the receding hairline sitting at the concert grand.

"Get up off that piano stool, you tomato," Willie snarled, "and let the real piano players take over."

George Gershwin laughed and obliged.

Willie sat down and plunged into one of his airy, sensitive compositions—the right hand tracing rainbows while the left made the rhythm undulate. Gershwin moved off, surrounded by admirers and goofy-drunk celebrity stalkers congratulating him on the recent success of *Rhapsody in Blue*.

At the bar, Tom and James P. watched Willie and doubtless had a belly chuckle. James P. might have wagged his head and commented on Willie's bloodthirsty rhetoric and pussycat musicianship. Tom might have looked over to where Gershwin was sitting on a sofa, his face partly obscured by the tuxedo trousers of the men standing around him and the bare shoulders of the gowned women leaning over him. And Tom might have noticed the studious look on Gershwin's face as Willie was playing. Tom had seen that look before, when the boy wonder of modern American composition had come up to Harlem and paid his fifty cents at the door to be admitted to "rent parties."

In the cruelly overcrowded conditions of most Harlem apartment buildings, there were often four or five people to a room meant for two. The rents were beyond the means of most of the tenants, so to be able to look the landlord in the eye come monthly judgment day, the Harlemites devised a novel and pleasant means of raising the required cash. The tenants of a building would pool their money and write a budget. Most of the capital expenditure was for food—pigs' feet, fried chicken, and other culinary delights of southern blacks. A substantial amount was set aside for liquor. A smaller amount was reserved for entertainment, and further sums were earmarked for advertising and for the services of a bouncer if things got rough. Word was spread through the neighborhood and to a select list of friends and relatives. Cards were printed, giving the location, describing the menu, and listing the names of the "professors of piano" who would be playing.

Guests arriving at a rent party would pay an admission charge, ranging from a dime to fifty cents. Once inside, they could buy food and liquor at reasonable prices and dance as much as they wanted to while the professors engaged in musical duels.

Rent parties would last as long as the guests and the refreshments held out, or until the needed rent money was raised. For many years the "rent social" was a successful and happy function in Harlem, as in other black communities in major cities. Waller was introduced to these socials by Johnson and Smith and quickly became one of the most popular pianists on the "chitlin' circuit." Rent parties were hard work, for all their fun; pianists used them as a kind of gymnasium to develop their stamina and their improvisational talents. They were almost forced to do so because of the fierce competition among pianists. A professor sitting down to the keyboard might play as many as thirty choruses on a tune before going on to his next selection, the object being to display his prowess and keep the other fellows away from the keys as long as possible. In his memoirs Willie the Lion recalled that it was not unusual for a pianist to play seven hours with only brief rests, and that some Harlem keyboard men became so caught up in the artistic and physical rigors of the chitlin' circuit that they thought of nothing else, possibly sacrificing broader careers.

Rent socials could be rowdy at times—Prohibition liquor was ghastly stuff designed to scatter the brains of the drinker as quickly as possible—and the police were sometimes called by unhappy neighbors. But more often than not a patrolman sent to quell the carousing was welcomed into the revelers' domicile and given a tumbler of gin, a plate of chicken, and a comfortable chair in the corner.

Waller's own comment on rent parties came late in his recording career with his hilarious *The Joint Is Jumpin'*, in which he recreated the atmosphere, inviting friends into the studio to simulate the giddy, noisy folderol as he sang:

> Check your weapons at the door
> Be sure to pay your quarter
> Drag your body on the floor
> Grab anybody's daughter
> The roof is rockin'
> The neighbors knockin'
> We're all bums when the wagon comes
> I said the joint is jumpin'.
>
> . . . .
>
> I got bail as we go to jail
> I said the joint is jumpin'.
> (Spoken): Don't give your right name—no no no.

Waller was probably first booked at a rent party in 1922. A few days before the engagement he was surprised, while walking down a Harlem street with Johnson, to hear a man he didn't know call, "Hey, Fats!" Tom nodded back and asked Johnson how the man could have known him. Johnson replied that the man was handing out cards for an upcoming rent party and that Waller's name was undoubtedly on them. Surprised and delighted, Fats walked back to the man and took one of the cards as a souvenir.

In 1922 Tom was a rapidly developing pianist with evident talent and drive, but he was still relatively inexperienced. To compensate, he began to sing and mug and crack jokes— Waller's ultimate gift may have been, not music, but his wonderful talent for companionship.

Waller's voice was an acceptable baritone, but it was seldom heard in its natural form. He most often rasped when he sang, or vocalized through his nose instead of his throat. Though he is legendary for the cheery violence he could do to lyrics he disliked, and fondly remembered for his clowning with rhythm songs, there are a few recordings of Waller singing relatively seriously, and in these he showed delicate and elegant phrasing.

At his rent-social bookings, a tune Waller frequently sang was *The Boy in the Boat,* a familiar pornographic ditty with dozens of verses accumulated over the years. At this early time, he must have also developed his way of injecting his spoken comments on the lyrics of popular tunes, a technique of his showmanship that in later years was largely responsible for his stardom.

Waller became more popular and accomplished on the chitlin' circuit at about the time white musicians, hearing of the pianistic feats on display at rent parties, began coming uptown to listen and learn. Among them was George Gershwin, who very early in his career wrote an unsuccessful one-act opera, *135th Street,* which attempted to capture the life tempo of Harlem and was a prototype for *Porgy and Bess.* Gershwin was already a successful popular songwriter and composer of scores for stage musicals, fascinated and attracted by black rhythm and syncopation schemes. He frequently dropped in on Harlem rent parties and spent his time sitting on the floor gazing up at James P. and Willie the Lion, and young Waller.

It was Gershwin who invited the Harlem trio to several Park Avenue soirees, and he had good reasons for bowing to Willie The Lion's taunt. Gershwin was not a considerable pianist, despite his melodic gifts; his tempo was wayward, and his playing didactic. He used the piano to demonstrate his ideas rather than to express them.

But Gershwin's admiration for Johnson, Smith, and Waller was not based on any feelings of inferiority as a keyboardist (his ego would not permit such feelings). What attracted Gershwin to the Harlem trio—especially to Johnson and Smith, since Waller was still a babe—was that they did exactly what he did. They were not, in his estimation, any more "jazz" players than he was, though they used syncopation and jazz technique. Gershwin was thrilled and delighted by Johnson, Smith, and Waller because they were melodists of extraordinary caliber, because their compositions were concertos of variations on a theme, and because in performance these variations were presented in *concert* form. Gershwin had concerts of his works performed in respectable halls; Smith, Johnson, and Waller presented theirs at rent parties. But the idea, the meaning, the content, and the effect were similar. The Harlem trio and Gershwin were modern American composers who had arrived at the same musical conclusions independently.

So Gershwin not only invited the trio to a party celebrating his triumph with *Rhapsody in Blue* (hurriedly composed between theatrical score assignments), but introduced them to his associates, such as Irving Berlin, bandleader Paul Whiteman, and Gershwin's brother-in-law Leopold Godowski, a pianist with whom Waller sometimes studied.

The trio received further engagements on the Park Avenue circuit, sometimes for free food and drink and sometimes for a flat fee. Willie the Lion remembered:

> We used to get bugged by some of the people we'd wind up playing for, but they'd always keep the juices flowing.
>
> They were always asking us silly questions. "Do you play by notes? Can you read music? Where were you born? How did you get into the music racket?" . . . We felt like a couple of whores being interviewed by a high school reporter.

A most generous hostess the trio performed for was the second Mrs. Harrison Williams. Her husband, director of a number of electric light and power companies, had been widowed in 1920. When he married Mona Strader Bush of Lexington, Kentucky, in 1926, his bride brought gaiety into his life. She invited songwriters and publishers to her parties, and the Williamses changed houses three times in three years, from East Seventy-second Street to Fifth Avenue and thence to Madison Avenue. Willie recalled:

> At [her] parties we felt more like teachers. Show business celebrities would study our work and try to get our music-arranging ideas. . . . Sometimes the artists who tried to pick up on some of our stuff had a hard time of it. James P. . . . wasn't a talker at all. He just played but couldn't explain what he was doing. They always thought they could get a lot out of Fats if they kept the jug handy, but when Fats got swinging he would sing and play for hours without saying anything sensible.

But the occasional pay from rent parties or Park Avenue affairs wasn't sufficient to meet Waller's already chronic spendthrift ways. About the same time as his appearance at the Gershwin celebration, he had published his first compositions. So began the baffling and often hilarious history of his relations with music publishers.

In 1924 Waller went to New England on a vaudeville tour as pianist for a group called Liza & Her Shufflin' Six. To while away the time between shows he pulled together some compositional ideas. His first tune was *Wildcat Blues*. The second was *Squeeze Me*, for which he was to become famous.

Squeeze Me was a patchwork affair rather than an original composition; Waller acted as editor rather than creator. The basic melody followed very closely the second theme of James P.'s *Fascination*. Waller's contribution was to take James' resolution of the second theme and expand it as a descending modulation. *Squeeze Me* is also supposed to have been a variation on the lost bawdy melody, *The Boy in the Boat*, but what parts Waller took cannot be known. (Johnson, who also knew the melody, may have used part of it for his second theme in *Fascination*.)

Waller originally called his pastiche *The Boston Blues*, though it was by no means a blues. He played it for Clarence Williams, the black publisher, who saw the tune turn into one of his biggest hits since *Sister Kate*. *Squeeze Me* also inspired other publishers to issue fiats to their house writers to come up with imitations involving a descending modulation for the resolution.

At Williams' urging, Waller submitted dozens of compositions and received advance cash payments for them. Few of the tunes were actually published (if the Williams company archives still exist, it would be fascinating to have the collection of early Waller compositions). Though Williams liked and respected Waller and was happy to encourage him, Williams was a songsmith himself, and his efforts to get tunes recorded—the most effective way of plugging them—were largely reserved for his own material. Moreover, Williams could not depend on Waller to record the songs Williams had written, since Tom's recording career from 1924 to 1927 was sporadic. Still less could Williams depend on Waller to remember the tunes he had written—Tom was such a fast and prolific composer that he often forgot his own product. In 1932, when Waller visited Paris, he was asked by a French critic to play *Sweet Savannah Sue,* which he'd recorded in 1929. Waller had to confess that the tune escaped him.

Waller wrote for quick money and thought himself ahead of the game if he got a $25 or $50 cash advance on a song. He never thought about contracts protecting his creations or about long-term royalties. His carelessness with his talent was part of his day-to-day attitude toward living. Melodies came so easily to him that he may have believed for a time that he was actually outsmarting publishers. He is known to have toured the publishers' offices at 1619 Broadway, giving a cheery hello, sitting down at the piano, rippling off an improvisation, and claiming that it was something he had been working on studiously. On at least one occasion he sold the same tune to three different publishers and collected cash advances from each. These "tours" of 1619 Broadway were lucrative in the short run, but Waller lost heavily from them in the long run.

Publishers were quick to spot Waller's game and to realize his increasing dependence (especially after alimony problems from his first marriage haunted him) on the fast advance. They also saw that Waller was extraordinarily pliable when liquor was offered and that he foolishly signed contracts which committed him to provide much while receiving little. Not that Tom paid much attention to contracts—he would sign them with hearty bonhomie and then forget them.

In 1929 Waller made the greatest professional mistake of his life when he signed over his personal copyrights to many of his greatest tunes for the insanely low sum of $500. Nine years later, while playing an engagement at the Yacht Club on Fifty-second Street in New York, he burst into tears after playing *If I Had You* (not his own) and explained to sympathizers that he was thinking of millions of dollars in royalties that he'd signed away in his foolish youth.

But there was also right on the side of the publishers. Jack Robbins, who published *Rhapsody in Blue,* once commented that if he had either the advance money he'd given Waller on unfinished tunes, or the finished tunes, he could have been a millionaire once over. And publishers *did* push Waller's material. Clarence Williams—with his contacts in the recording industry—saw to it that Waller's *In Harlem's Araby* was recorded, in 1925, by a pickup band featuring the unique soprano saxophonist Sidney Bechet. In 1927 Louis Armstrong recorded two Waller compositions, *I'm Goin' Huntin'* and *Georgia Bo-Bo.* The latter got Louis in deep trouble. Armstrong was under contract to Okeh Records with his Hot Five band, but—in the common practice of those days—he used the Hot Five to make a date for a competitor, Vocalion Records, under the name Lil's Hot Shots (Armstrong's wife, Lil Hardin, was the pianist in the combo). The performance features a thrilling shout vocal by Armstrong and a fine solo by trombonist Edward "Kid" Ory.

The trouble came because Louis was so unmistakably himself, and the Hot Five records were doing so well for Okeh that the Okeh label manager, Tommy Rockwell, hauled Armstrong into his office and gave him hell for aiding a competitor. Rockwell played the offending disc and dared Louis to deny his wickedness. Armstrong's reply was ingenious and contrite. "Gee, I don't know who made that record—but I'll never do it again!"

6

Soothin' Syrup Stomp

Tom Waller was one of history's great guzzlers. The exact date of his introduction to the pleasures and griefs of yeast, hops, and grapes is not precisely known, but it was certainly early in his life. A measured guess would be that, in the company of musicians and showfolk, Tom sipped his first taste about the time he was sixteen. As his musical services became more called for, and as he became a regular part of the high-living, select company of notable pianists, his drinking increased, so that by the age of eighteen he was able to hold his liquor and still have room for more. His capacity and desire for alcohol became dangerous shortly thereafter, as a reaction to his mother's death.

That Waller downed a gargantuan amount of hooch, both ersatz and bonded, during the rest of his life surely contributed to his own early passing. But his genial boozing added mightily to his legend. Eugene "Honeybear" Sedric, Waller's saxophonist, once declared: "Fats was drunk for eighteen years." Going on Sedric's calculations, this means that Waller was consistently in some sort of woozy state for 6,570 days, or 157,448 hours. But Waller's colossal, sustained quaffing had one beneficial side effect: seldom within view-halloo distance of sobriety, he suffered few hangovers.

Upon arising, at whatever hour his day might begin, Waller knocked back three fingers' worth of whiskey. This he described as his "liquid ham and eggs." Waller's lunches and dinners were composed of varied juices. His son Ronald, by his second wife, was once asked at school what his father's occupation was. The lad could only reply—honestly and with bewilderment and awe—"He drinks gin."

A few years before his death, Waller was vehemently charged by a doctor to temper his drinking habits. The composer, in a rare moment of common sense, took the warning seriously, compared it to his self-knowledge, hoped for the best, and attempted to form a meaningful relationship with soda pop. This he ordered by the case. But he found the mixture of syrup and carbonated waters to be pale maidens for his dalliance, so he soon switched to cases of wine. After a month or so, he divorced the grape and went back to his sweetheart, whiskey.

It should be mentioned that Waller was a great drinker not only in the amounts he consumed but also in the way liquor affected him. He was never nasty or hostile, and seldom maudlin. He came to happy terms with drinking: he wanted to be carefree and generous, and a good load of "Grandfather" (Old Grandad, his favorite bourbon) only gave him more impulse to be so. Waller wanted to live at the peak of existence, and not the least of his achievements was that he managed to be so continuously fuzzy and loose and yet so precisely disciplined in his music. Freedom in music can be had only through a willing submission to its rules, and a tasteful instinct as to when those rules should be bent or broken. Sober musicians of talent have wrestled for their entire careers with the question of when they should play by the book and when they should throw the book away. Waller never had to face that dilemma. Liquor didn't free him. It simply made his expression of freedom that much more pleasant.

Waller would have been one of the great comrades of history without his sloshing, but his tosspot camaraderie only made sweet moments sweeter. Louis Armstrong wrote:

I've seen Fats Waller enter a place, and all the people in the joint (I mean the place) would just rave and you could see a sort of gladness in their faces . . . honest . . . and Fats wouldn't be in the place a hot minute before he would tell them a fine joke and have everybody holding their sides from laughter . . . "Haw haw haw haw, he kills me."

Waller's entrance into any room betokened joy; he was a year-round Santa Claus. Standing five feet ten inches and weighing, in his words, "two hundred and eighty-five pounds of jam, jive, and *everything,*" he brought instant smiles and affection. There are few people in the world whose talent is to bring instant gladness, and it is that part of Waller's genius that has most sustained the tale of his life. Waller graced the planet by his living; he gave the human race a good reputation.

Musician Danny Barker remembered a litany that Waller spoke whenever he encountered a friend or acquaintance:

> How ya doin'? Good to see ya!
> How's your family?
> How's your wife?
> How's your cousin?
> How's your landlord?
> How's your undertaker?
> You're lookin' real prosperous—
> But you're gettin' uglier every day!

Waller made no secret of his drinking, although he didn't trade on it. He was a direct man, and sham was not in his nature. During a stage appearance Tom's brother-in-law Lewis Rutherford entered with a tray of bottles and glasses and Waller roared: "Awwww! Here's the man with the dream wagon. I want it to hit me around the edges and get to every pound." He meant the audience to have as good a time as he was having, and he meant to show them that when he played music he wasn't "working"—he was doing what he liked, and a little libation never hurt.

It is remarkable that with all the homicidal hooch Waller consumed before 1933 (when the Prohibition Amendment to the

Constitution was repealed), and with all the legal liquid he downed for ten years after that, the libations didn't begin to hurt until toward the end of his life. Willie the Lion recalled:

> In those days [1924] I had to almost push Fats down on the stool to get him to play. Young Waller was really a very shy kid, and I think it was that shyness that eventually turned him into such a heavy drinker.
>   . . . he was a mama's boy, at least when I first knew him, and his life got all jumbled up at the time of her death.

Tom disguised the jumbling with bonhomie and bacchanal. But he was always able to call on the juices of his distillery of talent. In 1929 Eddie Condon, banjoist and band organizer, was retained by Victor Records to bring Waller and a rehearsed band into the studios. Condon went to Harlem and found Waller expansive, genial, and woozy. Condon explained his mission and emphasized how important it was that Waller should convince the Victor staff that he was reliable and austere. To all of Condon's pleadings, Tom responded, "Fine, wonderful, perfect! Let's have a gin and talk about it." Condon, who was not unused to drinking, found himself on a merry-go-round of happy wassail that exhausted him. Three days later, still trying to make Waller focus on the importance of the upcoming record date, Condon woke up to see Tom happily snoring. In a panic, Condon realized that the record date was only hours away. Shaking Tom awake and desperately pleading the urgency of the moment, Condon was given a smile and an instruction: "Fine, wonderful, perfect! Give me some nickels so I can make the telephone go."

Condon supplied the coins. Waller phoned a cornetist, a clarinetist, and a trombonist and told them to meet him on a specified corner. When the musicians assembled, Waller bundled them all into a taxi. Condon gave the address of the studio. Tom, sitting in the front seat, turned around and wagged a finger at the adventurers. He outlined two melodies on the spot, humming them, and then hummed the harmony and counterpoint. All—including Condon—nodded agreement and understanding.

The quintet walked into the studio, Condon glancing nervously at the assembled executives. Waller sat at the piano. The recording engineer gave the signal to start, and the quintet charged into the first tune at a boiling pace. Condon had wondered about the absence of a drummer and a bassist, but "when I heard Waller's left hand I knew we didn't need them." Two minutes later the group had finished cutting a classic of hot jazz. The second tune was a blues.

The executives beamed and made nice noises, interspersed with pontifical comments about the virtues of well-rehearsed bands. Condon was paid his consultant's fee, and to cap the happy idiocy of the whole adventure the record was released with the titles (which Waller named on the spot) reversed. The slow blues was supposed to be *The Minor Drag,* and the hot number *Harlem Fuss.* The Victor staff bumbled and switched them, yet it is not impossible to find an after-the-fact justification for the switch. A blues could, after all, be a "fuss," and portions of the hot number, especially in Waller's solo, make good use of minor chords. As with all situations touched by Waller's giddy gifts, this joyous and haphazard record date was fine, wonderful, perfect.

The *Harlem Fuss* recording session was more or less typical of Waller record dates in the 1920s and early 1930s. Pulling himself together at the last possible minute, Waller called on his enormous reserves of creative ingenuity and crisp technique to perform creditably and often brilliantly under the most haphazard of circumstances.

Recording dates of that era by pickup groups were "grapevine" affairs. A music publisher wanted a song waxed and contacted a label. If the tune was a novelty number or a blues or a "hot" item, suitable jazz musicians were recruited. The label or the publisher sent out word to a reliable musician who could assemble enough of his peers for the specific needs of the date (a five-piece blues combo for a vocalist, a ten-piece "orchestra" for a pop tune, trios, quartets, and so on). Sheet music was provided by the publishers, who hoped that at least one of the gathered musicians could read; if not, a "house" pianist on call for the label or publisher was sent over to play the number through until the musicians had it down. There followed brief discussions about "head" arrangements (made up on the spot), and the session proceeded forthwith.

Tom Waller had been making records since 1922 as accompanist, soloist, band member, and nominal band leader. He was a successful songwriter and had contacts among record label personnel. He could read, and he was "reliable" in that, even if he didn't show up on time, he was an "instant study" and could galvanize a session by his efforts and his personality. He was popular with recording directors and engineers, who were never quite sure how much of his gusto was *joie de vivre* and how much was due to the amount of distilled waters consumed, but he made a substantial number of records between 1922 and 1934 (the year of his stardom). His early career is one of the best documented, on recordings, in all jazz.

As Mike Lipskin points out:

> His being a star was a kind of accident. Nobody had any idea that he was going to be that big, least of all him. He never looked for it; it just happened to him. If it hadn't happened to him, he could still have earned a very good living as a sideman on record dates, even without the songs he wrote. He could read, he was a good arranger, he could make guys want to play on a session—make they happy while they were doing it—and they had to record a lot of junk material. Fats could play any kind of a tune, on the organ or the piano. If it was a good tune, he made sure it got a proper reading. If it was a bad tune, he made it sound better than it was. That kind of guy, to a recording director, is invaluable. Nobody could have ever heard of the famous Fats Waller, and he still would have been one of the busiest musicians in the country—even today, if he'd lived.

Waller also had a particularly delicate sense of how to satisfy the requirements of a specific record date while satisfying his own musical sensibilities. He could play low-down and crudely when the occasion demanded, play politely and with delicate restraint, or let loose and howl. He had an instinct for knowing what the recording director, the label, and the publisher wanted, but also for knowing what the guys in the band wanted.

In the late 1920s Waller made a series of records with Morris' Hot Babies, a quintet led by the stiff and unimaginative trumpeter Thomas Morris. The format of the sessions was neo-New Orleans black Dixieland jazz, meant to sound as "Negro" as possible. The band was incapable of any subtlety, but Waller— doubling on piano and organ and playing well under his capacity—almost makes them sound rough and ready. His presence in the ensemble portions is volcanic. He uses the organ as a surprising sound, playing crude blues patterns with a gentle and brainy touch, as if he were Bach saying, "This is what I do on my day off," and his piano solos on such folk-blues tunes as *Please Take Me Out of Jail* and *Geechee* are witty imitations of whorehouse "professors." Some of the Morris dates throw in a gratuitous "Charleston" dance rhythm now and then so as to be up-to-date, and it must have been pleasing to Waller to hear how his patron, teacher, and friend James P. Johnson was being commercially honored—for James P. was the composer of *The Charleston,* which became *the* dance of "flaming youth" in America and Europe in the 1920s.[8]

Don Redman, clarinetist, saxophonist, and free-lance arranger, who had won fame for the charts he wrote for the great Fletcher Henderson Orchestra, was assigned to pep up the recordings of McKinney's Cotton Pickers, a black dance orchestra from Detroit. The dates were to be done in New York, and Redman brought in local experts, including cornetist Joe Smith (no relation to the "Empress of the Blues," Bessie Smith, but she preferred his warm tone to Louis Armstrong's dazzle as accompanist on many of her recordings) and Waller. Two of the tunes cut were Redman's own *That's the Way I Feel Today* and *Gee, Baby, Ain't I Good to You,* on both of which Waller played with restraint but grace, as befitted Redman's melodies and the

---

[8]Willie the Lion remembered that in the early 1900s when he and James P. were among the numerous pianists playing in saloons and in waterfront "dance academies," the clientele consisted mostly of black dockworkers, "Gullahs" from the Carolinas and "Geechies" from Georgia. According to Willie, the pianists improvised to spontaneous dance steps by the customers. James P. published the variations as *The Charleston.* It was inserted into his 1923 Broadway musical *Runnin' Wild* and became a sensation almost immediately.

capabilities of the Pickers, who were all read-the-little-black-dots-on-the-paper musicians.

Six months after the *Harlem Fuss/Minor Drag* session in September 1929 Waller was bundled together with a notable group of white and black players (one of the early biracial record dates), which included Otto Hardwick from Duke Ellington's band, Eddie Condon, the superb trombonist Jack Teagarden (not long arrived from Texas), and the young Gene Krupa. The group recorded two Waller tunes, probably hastily dashed off for a quick advance from a publisher who might well have demanded that Tom record the tunes before he forgot them: *Lookin' Good but Feelin' Bad* and *I Need Someone like You.* The first is a bouncy, sassy, citywise tune with lyrics by one of the three Santly brothers (which one is unknown)— Henry, Joseph H., or Joe. Possibly Joe, who wrote *Big Butter and Egg Man* and *At the Moving Picture Ball,* provided the words, sung by The Four Wanderers, with Waller taking a no-nonsense solo and supporting the vocal quartet with boiling rhythm. *I Need Someone like You* is one of Waller's many shy and ethereal tunes, heavily disguised by a bumpety-bump rendering, but *Lookin' Good* contains a fine, wild Teagarden solo and trumpeter Leonard Davis, an Armstrong disciple with happy energy, gets as close to his master as he can.

In 1931 Waller appeared on three sides by Ted Lewis & His Orchestra. Lewis was a vaudevillian and amateur clarinetist, a performer whose lazy vocals and professional dispensing of cheer sounded rather like a village druggist recommending aspirin for all ills. Lewis' tag line, famous in his day, was: "Is everybody happy?"—pronounced "Is *ehhvvv*-ree-*bod*-eh hahp-*ayyy?*" The Great Depression of the 1930s affected musicians as much as anyone else, so it is not surprising that Lewis' band contained four jazz notables, glad to have a job because the popular Lewis could pay salaries: Muggsy Spanier from Chicago, a hot cornet devoted to Armstrong; George Brunies, elder statesman of the trombone from his time, in the early 1920s, with one of the first great jazz bands, the New Orleans Rhythm Kings; Don Murray, clarinetist, veteran of the superb Jean Goldkette Orchestra and sometime pal of the divine and doomed

Bix Beiderbecke; and Benny Goodman, the future "King of Swing," a clarinetist with few ideas of his own, whose talent was to synthesize the ideas, tones, and styles of every superior clarinetist, white or black, and explain them through his technique.

I'm Crazy about My Baby, Dallas Blues (the first published blues, 1912), and *Royal Garden Blues* are perfect examples of how Waller's presence could assure that proceedings conducted with commercial intent could still be memorable.

Tom was called in to provide spark, and the tunes are largely given over to him. *I'm Crazy about My Baby* was his own tune. He sang it straight and lazily sentimental. *Dallas Blues,* shows him formally trying to sing a blues, a form for which he was unsuited and in which he had little interest; his piano solo is interrupted by Lewis' spoken interjections ("Play it boy, play it . . . that's niiiiiiiiiiice"). But in *Royal Garden Blues,* an upbeat number, we have perhaps the only example of Waller growling and biting and tearing into a vocal as if he really meant to sing a blues.

Tom's presence is obviously inspiring to Muggsy Spanier, who plays one of those tight, muted choruses for which he was ideal in *Royal Garden,* and Brunies—never an ambitious trombonist—performs as though remembering his heady young days with the Rhythm Kings. Goodman, given the assignment of pretending to be Lewis on the clarinet, is calculating but cautiously enthusiastic.

In much more relaxed circumstances, Waller appeared as a guest soloist on four dates by a semi-big band led by Jack Teagarden, in 1931, "Mr. T.," in addition to being the finest jazz trombonist who ever lived, was a warm and engaging vocalist. He was as mellow as Waller was abrasive and jabbing. On *I'll Be Glad When You're Dead, You Rascal You* and *That's What I Like about You,* Teagarden takes the vocals while Waller shouts out spoken comments. Mr. T. is so obviously delighted to have Waller on the date that he comes close to dissolving into joyful laughter—there are moments when Teagarden is fighting for control to restrain himself from a glorious guffaw. The opening dialogue of *That's What I Like about You,* a tune about a fellow getting around to proposing marriage because he and his girl have so much in common, Teagarden and Waller have a spoken exchange which ridicules the whole idea of the song, Teagarden taking the swain's part and Waller the fair maiden's. The exchange ends with Teagarden complaining: "You're big and fat!" And Waller, as the prospective bride, yelps with mock-offended female dignity: "Don't talk about my velocity!"

Musicians knew and respected the velocity of Waller's talents. In a few years the public would applaud his girth, his personality, and his music, making him a star, and Tom Waller would continue one of the longest and most creative benders in the annals of the planet. In the mid- and late-1930s, he and his manager, W. T. "Ed" Kirkeby, practiced a question-and-answer routine at the beginnings of recording sessions, as if to invoke the blessings of Bacchus on the proceedings. Sitting in the studio control room, Kirkeby would watch Waller making significant progress on a fifth of "Grandfather" and call out:

"Tom, is that your last drink?"

And Waller would gaily reply: "No, sir, Mr. Kirkeby, that's my first bottle."

Then, addressing the piano, Tom worked his magic.

7
Keepin' Out of Mischief Now

FROM THE MID-1920s until the day he died, Tom Waller was the object of keen and diligent pursuit by shyster lawyers and shoddy process servers who attempted to tag him with legal papers commanding him to appear in court to answer charges of defaulting on alimony payments.

Tom's marriage to Edith Hatchett in the early 1920s was a direct result of his longing for supportive female companionship after his mother's death. The couple moved in with Edith's parents at first but occupied their own lodgings thereafter. At best, the union might have developed into a cordial and convenient relationship, with the partners showing consideration for each other while not being truly interested in each other. But Tom's musical career took fire not long after the vows were pronounced; in the midst of lessons with James P., engagements at saloons and clubs, recording dates, and occasional tours, there was little time for Tom to attend to his marriage or seriously consider the role of husband.

The couple separated a few years after their marriage, and a divorce was processed. Tom's attitude seems to have been that he had made an emotional mistake and that the experience of his marriage was punishment enough for his error. Edith Hatchett-Waller's attitude was, understandably, quite different; she and her son, Thomas Waller, Jr., had to be supported. The subject of alimony quickly became a sore point between Tom and his ex-spouse. It could not, perhaps, have been otherwise. After making initial payments, Tom was more than lax in meeting his legal obligations (he was never astute with money in any situation), and Edith Hatchett-Waller, financially desperate, called in the law.

So began the Great Waller Chase, sometimes hilarious, sometimes humiliating, with legions of small-fry barristers sneaking and galloping after the musician. These harassments had a dangerous effect on his career in the late 1920s, when, after a straitjacket ruling from a judge and threats of protracted imprisonment, most of the money he earned was going to retroactive alimony payments. Waller's reaction was to miss recording dates and to curtail his activities because he could not bear the idea of working, in effect, for his ex-wife. (He missed several Victor dates, which prompted the Victor staff to assign Eddie Condon as a troubleshooter for the 1929 *Minor Drag*/*Harlem Fuss* session previously described.)

There were several notable battle scenes in Waller's alimony wars. One took place in 1927, when Waller was hauled into court and sternly admonished by the judge, who offered to defer putting Tom in the hoosegow if he would agree to abide by the payment schedule. Tom agreed. The judge told him to go in peace and meet his bills. Edward Martin Waller was in the courtroom. Tom hugged his father, who gave him a pat on the shoulder. This is the only recorded instance of anything resembling affection between the austere Edward Martin and his openhearted son.

On another occasion Waller was again before the bench. Unknown to him, several of his musician pals had prevailed upon a nonmusical acquaintance who was a boyhood chum of the magistrate to intercede on Tom's behalf.

"Ha—hum," said the judge. "Your name is Thomas Waller?"

"Yes, sir, Your Honor."

The lawgiver looked at a sheaf of papers before him and squinted, as if in deep concentration.

"Case dismissed—ha, hum."

Waller was not always so lucky. He was jailed at least twice for failure to pay what he called "my back house dues." In one instance, friends raised $500 bail and dashed to the pokey to rescue Tom from durance vile. They found him reluctant to leave. His cellmate was a millionaire who, like Tom, preferred to do time rather than feed his ex-wife. The millionaire, spreading a little joy among the guards, had contrived to install an upright piano in the cage and to have gourmet meals, decent whiskey, and cigars sent in.

"Come back later," Waller told his buddies. "*Much* later."

In 1929 Waller faced a fire-and-brimstone judge who sentenced him to a protracted term on the misnamed Welfare Island (now Roosevelt Island), a lonely and dismal spot in the East River. During this spell in the slams, Waller's father died. Since Tom was a youngster, Edward Martin had made holy mumblings about jazz being the Devil's path to woe and disgrace; now it appeared that his prophecies had come true.

Rescue from prison came when bail was supplied by Gene Austin, the first "crooner" and the most popular singer of the twenties. His recording of *My Blue Heaven* swept the country in the early 1920s, and he continued to be a bestselling recording artist. Austin liked to go uptown to look in on Harlem rent parties and had busted a few jugs with Willie the Lion. When Waller was brought into court and the judge demanded to know why he should accept bail, Austin spun a tale of an upcoming recording session for which Tom's piano talents were essential; the crooner intimated that without Waller the date couldn't take place, which would put other musicians out of work. The judge agreed to accept bail, but gave Tom a verbal dusting before freeing him.

Waller discographies list a November 25, 1929, recording session under Austin's name. The tune performed was *My Fate Is in Your Hands,* with music by Waller and lyrics by Andy Razaf, his principal collaborator. The title is said to have come from Razaf's pleas to a traffic cop when he and Waller were stopped for speeding and the police officer prepared to write out a ticket for a heavy fine.

Though Tom avoided court in his later years, he was always somewhat in arrears on his "back house dues," and had to keep a constant lookout for the seedy advocates who attempted to serve him with papers. These assaults came both in New York and out of town. By the mid-1930s Tom could not only "smell law" from a distance but had trained the members of his band to do so. The cue for a fast Waller exit was the line: "Here comes the man with the paper." On those occasions when Tom couldn't get off the bandstand quickly enough, he and his group would try to baffle the legal gleaners by talking in a mock Caribbean accent.

The shyster would approach the stage with a let's-foreclose-on-the-farm grin and inquire, "Say, I've got a message for Fats Waller. You must be him."

Eyes wide and innocent, a cigarette dangling from his lower lip, Tom would say something on the order of: "Me Fahts? Naw, sihr. Him biggah—*much* biggah—dan me. I not *faht,* mahn, me just roly-poly, you know?"

After his 1929 incarceration, however, Tom was sufficiently chagrined to make some of his payments on time, albeit without grace, for a special reason. Not long after his divorce, he met and fell in love with Anita Rutherford. They were married in 1927 after a brief courtship, on the understanding that Waller would meet his debts. Waller also received advice from his manager of the time, "Captain" George Gaines, a theatrical press agent, to put his life into some semblance of order.

To meet his alimony payments, which necessitated a reliable income flow, Tom lowered his price as a tunesmith. He is known to have offered to dash off a ditty for a publisher and set a selling price of $2.50.

Waller's casual attitude toward the long-range value of his compositions was disastrously displayed in 1929, when he sold the copyrights for nearly thirty songs—including *Ain't Misbehavin'* and *Honeysuckle Rose*—for a paltry $500. It was the greatest professional mistake of his life.

The sale of his treasures becomes even more awful when one

considers the quality of the melodies. Nearly every Waller tune had not only strength and flexibility but contained fascinating and delightful subthemes and harmonies. Waller's compositions were deceptively simple; they were like polished mahogany, in that the veneer was immediately appealing but the quality of the piece was disclosed by a study of the grains. Most of Waller's solo piano recordings of his tunes—especially a fruitful series of sessions in 1929, recorded in a converted Camden, New Jersey, church with superb acoustics—give a hint of the wonderful potential of the inner themes of his compositions. But it was sometimes left for other musicians, operating in different circumstances and without Tom's chronic need of quick money, to explore those inner themes and pay more attention to them than Waller was able to do.

Three great musicians who exercised this opportunity with Waller compositions were his friends Louis Armstrong and Duke Ellington and the legendary white cornetist and pianist Bix Beiderbecke.

In 1928 Armstrong (with Earl Hines on piano) cut *Squeeze Me*. The performance is taken at the mid-tempo which is correct for the tune, and Armstrong sings a "scat" vocal chorus that mines and refines the inner workings of the melody, evoking all its harmonic and improvisational potential while remaining faithful to the tender, slightly shy emotional intent of the composition.

In July 1929, young Duke Ellington and the first of his great orchestras recorded *Black and Blue* and *Jungle Jamboree*. The latter was a variation on *Tiger Rag*. The former was written by Waller with Andy Razaf for a Harlem nightclub floor show. The producer of the revue told Waller and Razaf that the show needed an interpolated number, a scene of a black girl in bed moaning over the trials of being a black, and that the tune and lyrics should be "funny." Waller and Razaf didn't see anything humorous in the assignment. Tom composed a *via dolorosa* melody, while Razaf wrote lyrics that made a statement for the whole race and its place in society: "What did I do/To be so black and blue?"

Ellington's recording contained the rich orchestral voicings for which he was known at that time—and for which he would later become famous and respected—but his arrangement of the composition was spare and bare, as befitted the intent of the melody. Cast in minor chords, *Black and Blue* is a triumph of composition in its balance of the sweet and the bitter, with an undertone of anger being born.

Bix Beiderbecke was the boy-god of 1920s jazz, the first white musician to attract and interest black players. He began as a piano prodigy at the age of five in Davenport, Iowa. Though Bix's fame came from his unorthodox handling of the cornet— he preferred its intimate tone to the tone of the piercing trumpet, and his fingering relied on the traditionally "weak" third valve, which Bix converted into an asset—his musical thinking tended to center on the piano as the instrument of ultimate expression.

A portion of Bix's legend, apart from his drinking and early death, has to do with his piano studies, most of them written toward the end of his life. In his recording career there are only four examples of his piano playing, one of them being his famous composition *In a Mist* (1927), the prototype for much of the ambitions and the artistic claims of "modern" jazz.

The Bix piano recording of interest here is *Wringin' and Twistin'*, written by Waller and Frank Trambauer. "Tram" was a C-melody saxophonist and ambitious bandleader, whose career never quite caught fire; he was also Bix's companion and musical adviser. In 1927 both of them were featured in the Jean Goldkette Orchestra, operating out of Detroit. The Goldkette band played a booking at the Roseland Ballroom in New York, where the alternate orchestra was Fletcher Henderson's. As early as 1924, "Smack" Henderson, a brilliant arranger, had put together a band that could play sweet and hot, and had peopled it with such mighty talents as Louis Armstrong, cornetist Joe Smith, trombonists Charlie "Big" Green and Jimmy Harrison, and reedists Buster Bailey, Benny Carter, and Coleman Hawkins.

Henderson lived on "Striver's Row" in Harlem (the block of apartment buildings designed by Stanford White), where the small black middle class of the time made their homes. Early morning breakfasts for the band and guests were served by Henderson's wife, Leora, a genial, bulky woman who was a trumpeter and led an all-girl band. Bix and Tram were present at some of these breakfasts, as was Waller—who once wrote nine tunes for Henderson as barter for nine hamburgers.

Casual music—"noodling" in the then contemporary jazz term— was made at these Henderson breakfasts. White and black musicians demonstrated their ideas and techniques. Bix, who in 1927 was working out the structure of *In a Mist,* might have sat in on piano. Waller surely did, and among the musicians he jammed and noodled with was Frankie Trambauer. In September, Tram, Bix (on piano), and Eddie Lang, the great guitarist,[9] recorded *Wringin' and Twistin'.*

In October, Bix and Tram recorded with the rhythm section from Red Nichols and His Five Pennies[10] under the name of The Chicago Loopers, although the sessions were made in New York. The recordings were an attempt to beat the cautious and mechanical trumpeter Nichols at his own game. The combo played polite, low-volume jazz, and hoped to replace Nichols' studio group and pick up consistent and well-paying recording dates. The experiment was a commercial failure, but one of the tunes cut was Waller's *I'm More than Satisfied,* a delightful melody showing the youthful Waller in his prime. *I'm More than Satisfied,* which should be rescued from its oblivion, has the three marks of Tom's best compositions: strong construction, charm, and inner voicings with a potential to expand the composition from a readily digestible pop song to a concerto.

---

[9]Eddie Lang (Salvatore Massano), who took his professional name from that of a high school basketball hero in his home state of Pennsylvania, was so skilled and successful on the guitar that he caused the demise of the banjo as a jazz instrument. His association with the superb violinist and rakehell Joe Venuti resulted in their creation of "chamber-music jazz" in the 1920s. Their efforts directly inspired the collaboration of guitarist Django Reinhardt and violinist Stephane Grappelli in the Quintet of the Hot Club of France recordings of the 1930s.

[10]Nichols, a trumpeter of little personal imagination, took his tone, style, and ideas from Bix Beiderbecke, and Bix, who was normally an easygoing fellow, cordially disliked him for it.

Bix's cornet work on *I'm More than Satisfied*—it is the only time in the Loopers sessions where he sounds interested—is strongest on the final ensemble chorus. His accents and manipulation of tone pressure to show emotion are subtle, exciting, and poignant. Like Waller, Bix was best at expressing bruised innocence. Waller disguised his hurts with bravado and gusto; Bix's defense was in his discipline and classicist approach to purity of tone and cleanliness of execution. Both of them were fascinated with the harmonic possibilities of jazz; both came to the eventual conclusion that jazz—as it was understood at the time—restricted their talents and ambitions. Shortly before his death, Waller was embarking on what could have been a fabulous career as a composer for the Broadway musical theater. Bix spent his last years composing avant-garde piano tone poems. Waller complained late in his life that when he tried to play "some of that fine modern stuff" in a club, there would always come a bellow from a customer: "Hey, Fats—why don't you swing it?" whereupon Waller would resignedly holler back: "All right, man, here 'tis," and burst into the "jam, jive, and *everthin'*" that had made him a national figure.

Waller died at thirty-nine of drink and pneumonia; Bix, of the same causes, at twenty-eight. They were alike in many ways. Bix was a German Protestant with a Teutonic sense of duty and responsibility, and Tom was a lapsed yahoo Baptist; but both had been warned against jazz by fathers who refused to recognize or could not understand their sons' talents, and both had mothers who encouraged their genius. Tom's survival of the moonfaced white lad by eleven years was probably due to Waller's acceptance of the "mystery" (in the religious sense) of music; his acceptance of it was complete, visceral, animal. Bix looked for proofs of his faith in the mystery and for confidence in himself; unable to reconcile or juggle those abstractions, he destroyed himself. Tom Waller would also destroy himself, but he took longer to do it and had a better time for himself and his audience while doing it.

Tom's casual, negligent attitude toward the commercial and artistic value of his compositions, coupled with the exploitation of black composers by white (and black) music publishers of the

1920s, made him woeful and angry later on. He confided to friends and associates that some of the biggest hits of the twenties were, in fact, his own tunes, to which he had sold the copyrights and his identity as their composer. There can be little doubt that Waller's complaints were true. He was not a man given to claiming honors and accomplishments that were not due him.

Nor were Tom's copyright losses always at the hands of venal professional music publishers. Bill Challis, arranger for both the Jean Goldkette and Paul Whiteman orchestras, and the man who notated Bix Beiderbecke's piano tone poems, recalls:

> I went up to Harlem one day to Connie's Inn with Fletcher Henderson. He kept telling me, "There's this fellow that you've got to hear on the organ." We walked into the club, and this big black guy is sitting at the piano, playing. I thought he was good, but he wasn't doing anything that knocked me out. Fletcher said, "Wait 'til you hear him on the organ." Well, I did, a couple of days later, and Waller *did* knock me out. I had never heard—and nobody had at that time—the kinds of things that Waller was doing.
>
> Sometime later, I got a call from Fletcher. He said: "Listen, I have a tune here, and I want you to do an arrangement for it; I'll give you half the publishing." That sounded like a good deal to me, so I went up to where he was living with the arrangement manuscript and gave it to Leora. She was Fletcher's wife—a wonderful woman, big and round and jolly. I had used her as a copyist before. That was the last I heard about the tune, which was *D Major Blues*. Later on, Henderson recorded it, but I never saw any dough from it in royalties. Then—oh, this must have been twenty years later or thereabouts—I ran into Benny Carter, who was with the Henderson band at that time. We got to talking about the old days, and about "Smack" Henderson—and I mentioned to Buster this *D Major Blues* thing, which I had always thought was Henderson's tune. And Buster said right off the bat: "Oh, that was Fats Waller's."

No one can say for sure what tunes Waller dashed off to meet his hamburger debt, but the recordings of *Hot Mustard* and *Have It Ready* in 1926 and 1927 are very much in the Waller mode, and Henderson's solo on *Hot Mustard* is completely in the Waller style. Both compositions are credited to Henderson, yet "Smack" was not noted or celebrated as a composer but as a bandleader, arranger, and spotter of talent. Applying the Challis experience, it is fair to ask: What price glory? What price hamburger?

8

Never Heard of Such Stuff

Seldom have man and instrument been made for each other as Tom Waller was for the pipe organ, an instrument which, legend has it, derives from the syrinx, or panpipe, of ancient Greece. Pan was the frisky god of shepherds, a goat from his waist down and a man from the belly button up, who played such dulcet and heady tunes on his pipes that the sheep were passive and content. This left the shepherd ample time, under the inspiration of the music, to knock off a bladder gourd of wine and, there being an available maiden about, conduct her into yon forest for a meaningful discussion of animal husbandry.

Panpipes were also found in old China, where they were designed in the shape of phoenix wings, with the pipes separated into masculine and feminine tones. The organ, the eventual outcome of the panpipe, also made much of masculine and feminine tones, delivering both with such an acoustic thrust that the organ has traditionally been regarded as the lion of instruments.

Though its origins are secular, hedonistic, and profane, the organ is most familiar as a persuasive machine for sacred music. During the Middle, or Dark, Ages, most organs were built by monks and by workmen under their direction.

The organ continued to be primarily a religious instrument until the end of the ninteenth century, when man-made electricity, combined with pneumatics, inspired an Englishman, Robert Hope-Jones, to design a variation specifically intended for the performance of popular music, and later for the accompaniment of silent movies.

In the middle 1920s Tom Waller was coaxed over to the renovated Lafayette Theatre, away from his position at the Lincoln Theatre, by the offer of a more generous salary and the chance to play a Hope-Jones organ. He was uniquely fitted, by talent, background, and personality, to perform on an instrument whose history and development were such a mixture of sublime and sweaty lores and motives, so pagan and pure all at once—as Waller was.

There is no doubt that Tom Waller was reverent toward the pipe organ. He often said so, and in all his recordings on the "God-box" he sounds serious about what he is doing, even if what he is playing is pixie starshine. He was fascinated by the grandiose sound of the instrument and its overwhelming tonal (and, by extension, emotional) capabilities. While he displayed his mastery of the organ he also demonstrated, in his playing, just what kind of sweet monster he had tamed.

In 1927 Waller went to the Victor Talking Machine Company's studios in Camden, New Jersey, for two sessions, in January and February, which produced eight solos. Fifty years later they are still astonishing in their virtuosity, technical command, and imagination. Most of the tunes are Waller originals which, despite their period titles (*Hog Maw Stomp, Messin' Around with the Blues, Rusty Pail,* and so on), are polytheme compositions with the intricate delicacy of Joplin's or James P. Johnson's work, but delivered with a gusto and sass that are all Waller's.

At that time it was not thought possible that the organ could be used so well for jazz. There had been occasional recordings, usually in blues records, where a pianist might play the harmonium—the reed organ that sounded like an accordion with bronchitis—but these were crude chording efforts.

Thomas Waller virtually invented the pipe organ as a jazz

instrument, but his contribution to and domination of the machine were so great that, when he died, the role of the jazz organ mostly died along with him. No one could follow or duplicate his achievements with it; his association with the organ was a one-man art form, entirely dependent on his person. Though there have been good and interesting jazz organists since, none of them approached the machine with the same eagerness that Waller did, and none have been able to realize his fusion of his talents with the power of the monster. Jazz organists since Waller's time have tended to play berserkly in order to baffle the instrument, or have let the instrument baffle them.[11]

Waller's 1927 recordings also included accompaniments to vocals by Alberta Hunter on *Sugar, Beale Street Blues,* and *I'm Going to See My Ma,* with Waller recording solo versions of the first two numbers at the same May 20 session. In these, as in his solos earlier in the year, there is a running strain of wistfulness which comes close to melancholy, for Waller's organ playing always contained a good deal of gospel sentiment. This is not surprising, since Waller learned to play the harmonium as a boy after hearing his mother accompany family hymn singing on that instrument, and also saw her playing the organ at church services. When he was in England in 1938 for the first of his European tours he recorded a series of spirituals which have a thrilling majesty about them, but they are also demonstrations of an emotional man controlling strong emotions with difficulty. At one of the sessions he began to record *Abide with Me,* his mother's favorite hymn, but collapsed in tears when thinking of her death.

His 1943 recording of the spiritual *Sometimes I Feel like a Motherless Child* (virtually one of the last he made) is a blazing display of gospel fervor, jazz feeling, and something beyond both. He performs the feat of being faithful to the melody—he was, above all things, a melodist—while playing such variations

---

[11]With the invention of the portable electric organ, a boon to traveling musicians but a cheap imitation of the sound of the parent instrument, most of the tonal capabilities have been lost. The same holds true of the electric piano as opposed to a concert grand or a good upright—as chuck steak is to filet mignon. . . .

upon it that he recomposes or subcomposes the melody, turning it into an étude. To top it off, he speaks the title at the beginning of the record as though he were mocking the sentiments, and in the middle of the performance he reprises his wonderful wisecrack, "I wonder what the po' people are doin'. I'd love to be doin' it with 'em."

Solitude, by Duke Ellington, was recorded immediately after *Motherless Child,* and here Waller's humor, expressed in a haphazard, silly vocal, makes clearer why it was included. In the last year of his life, his awesome boozing had caught up with him, affecting not only his health but his emotional and musical thought. Motives and passions were jumbled and inconsistent; in the counterfeit bliss of being continually blotto, Waller was mixing his popular, jazz, religious, and personal musical thoughts into an accidental whole, disparate and contradictory in its elements but held loosely together by his personality and his disciplined musical technique.

Waller's last recordings were made when he was thirty-nine; his first extended recording session on the organ took place when he was twenty-three. To completely master the pipe organ at such an early age shows precocity; to transform the instrument and redefine it in terms of jazz—before jazz was accepted as a new standard of excellence—is flabbergasting. Perhaps the most apt comparison is that between Waller and Walt Whitman. Both converted "biblical" instruments (in Waller's case, the organ; in Whitman's, the prose rhythm of the New Testament) to uniquely personal vehicles not only of the religious impulse but of their own talents and individualities. Both were poets of the first order.

Waller's love of the organ was early and permanent. In the 1930s, when he was earning even more money than he, the profligate, could spend, he bought a portable organ and had it toted up to his hotel rooms while on the road. During a stay in Chicago, Lyon & Healy, a local musical instrument store, presented him with a baby Hammond as a promotional gesture. Later, Waller also had an organ in his house in Queens. It was his pleasure to reel in after a show, seat himself at his adored baby monster, and play until morning. Once while on tour, he invited musicians to his hotel room for a Christmas Eve party. Tom thought it would be a nice gesture, seeing that he and the musicians were all so far from home, to have a dawn gathering, drink the health of St. Nicholas several times, fool around, make music, and just generally be together. The guests arrived, and the libations were plentiful. There was much hilarity and banter. Then Tom began to play spirituals and Christmas carols on the organ, and before long everyone in the room, including Waller, was sobbing with thoughts of homes missed and loved ones far away. Tom's music could sometimes be a trifle too evocative.

Among the many apocryphal stories about Tom Waller's life and music is one, first printed in 1939, which tells that he recorded organ solos of various classical pieces, following them up with jazz versions, and that the records were suppressed on the demand of an RCA Victor classical—and white—organist whose ego couldn't stand the strain. It is a fine story, possibly true, and appealing because it teases with the faint hope that the legendary Waller classical/jazz sides may turn up someday through accident or diligent searching. There is no listing of such a session in the RCA files,[12] but even if the session took place, the masters have in all probability long since been destroyed, donated to "scrap metal" drives during World War II, or simply thrown out during a general housecleaning of "old" inventory undertaken by RCA Victor in the 1950s. Earl Hines—that superb pianist and Waller's friend—gave this opinion when told of the "lost" classical/jazz session: "If they had 'em in the vaults, then they sold 'em to the collectors."

One session which *almost* took place was recalled by Waller in 1943, during an interview with the *New York Times:* "I went down to Camden [New Jersey, where Victor maintained studios] with 'Pops'—that's Paul Whiteman—to make a recording of *Whispering.* They wanted me to play the organ like Jesse Craw-

---

[12]Neither in the files for recordings intended for general release nor in the files for custom recordings. "Custom" recordings are those paid for by the performers, usually amateurs. Waller is supposed to have done a "custom" session paid for by a Scot who was a jazz enthusiast and played "hot" bagpipes. Alas, this is another fine tale with no corroboration.

ford.[13] But why should I play like Crawford? I wanted to play like me. So there we were having one beaut of a dee-bate. So Bix says to me: 'Come on. Let's go over in a corner and shout this one down together.' Man, that Bix near drove me crazy. But we sure turned out a honey that day."

Of all the "lost" Waller sessions, the organ/cornet duet between two of the most poetic jazz artists is the most tantalizing. That it was played but not recorded—due to the cornflake commercial tastes of the recording director—is infuriating. But as Waller often remarked, "One never knows, do one?"

---

[13]Crawford was a popular commercial organist of the 1920s, and an acquaintance and admirer of Waller. Waller substituted for him annually at the Paramount Theatre, playing the Hope-Jones organ.

9

In Harlem's Araby

ALMOST FROM THE MOMENT that the Prohibition Amendment to
the Constitution went into effect in January 1920, a new type of
small businessman sprang up. Responding to public thirst and
public resentment toward a loony law passed by a cringing Congress at the behest of pressure groups of frumpy women and
shrill preachers, thousands of normally prudent folk became
bootleggers—suppliers of genuine and ersatz hooch.

In Harlem there were hundreds of retail outlets for illegal spir-
its, ranging from swanky nightclubs to corner cigar stores. One
of the outlets was the delicatessen owned by Connie and George
Immerman on 125th Street. (In 1920 Harlem was still a racially
mixed neighborhood, and 125th, so soon to become the main
promenade of the black community, was predominantly white.)

The Immermans ran a prosperous business, with their delivery
calls answered by young Tom Waller. After Prohibition came in,
those delivery calls increasingly included orders for "pickled
goods," "aged delights," or "grapes." Waller was dispatched with
these, the bottles being stuck in the inside pockets of a baggy
jacket draped around his broad and pudgy frame. On one occa-

sion, as he later recalled, he had just been loaded up when the door opened and two federal Prohibition agents swaggered in, flashing badges and displaying their pistols,[14] and announcing that they were there to conduct an investigation.

Waller edged toward the door. The agents demanded to know who he was. The Immermans identified Waller as their delivery boy. He was allowed to leave on his appointed rounds. Tom walked slowly, so as not to let the bottles clink.

Years passed, and the Immermans' delivery boy turned into a local hero with his organ playing at the Lincoln Theatre. When the Frank Schiffman family[15] bought the Lincoln and renovated the Lafayette, installing Waller as the organist at the latter palace, this was part of a movement by owners of entertainment property to take advantage of an increased "downtown trade." With the hedonistic defiance of Prohibition among whites, there came a taste for the exotic, the taboo, and the generally frowned-upon. In New York, this attitude translated into a fascination with things black, and Harlem suddenly experienced a surge of downtown trade coming to see the comedians, dancers, and orchestras of their community.

The result was the opening of three major night spots and dozens of alley and basement joints, which provided entertainment ranging from the glorious to the despicable. Between 1923 and 1933 Harlem became the Port Said of the American East Coast. It was a fabulous time of talent, hoopla, and verve, and Waller was very much a part of it.

The Lafayette, where Waller was holding forth on the Robert Hope-Jones organ, was next to a dying club called the Shuffle Inn, named after the first all-black Broadway hit, *Shuffle Along* (1921), whose score was by Eubie Blake and Noble Sissle. The owners of the club offered the property to the Immermans, who refurbished the basement dugout and named it Connie's Inn. In

---

[14]The federal agents tended to be trigger-happy. In one year alone they killed 2,000 people, over half of whom were innocent (and largely nondrinking) citizens who got in the way of the bullets. The agents were also notoriously prone to drunkenness. Most of them were ruffians and slimy characters appointed by wooly-headed bureaucrats, and not a few were pathological cases.

[15]They also bought Hurtig & Seamon's Theatre, renaming it the Apollo.

1923 the club presented an extravagant floor show, *Keep Shuf-flin'*, which doubled during the early evening at a Broadway theater. Waller was a semiregular figure at the club; he had become such a local hero with his organ playing that a small Estey model, painted white, was installed for his convenience and pleasure whenever he happened to amble into Connie's. He had a standing invitation to play between orchestra sets, and he often took advantage of the welcome. He played as much for pleasure as for tips, but after October 1927, when he was fired from the Lafayette because he and his sweetheart, Anita Rutherford, did so much wooing and cooing on the organ bench that Waller forgot to pay attention to the keys, Connie's Inn was a source of much-needed income.

The two other leading Harlem night spots were Small's Paradise and the Cotton Club. Small's and Connie's were "black-and-tan" establishments where the races mingled. The Cotton Club excluded blacks, except for waiters and visiting celebrities, such as Bill "Bojangles" Robinson. The Cotton Club, where Duke Ellington's band was in residence for twelve years, was financed and controlled by downtown gangsters, principally Owney "The Killer" Madden, a British-born jackanape who by his teens was a veteran of the ferocious Gophers, one of the last of the old and terrible New York street gangs. With the arrival of Prohibition, Madden—who had a dead-man score of thirteen—found a lucrative living in the operation of a "cereal malt" company which peddled "Madden's No. 1 Beer."[16]

Among the larger and better-appointed clubs was Barron's, owned by Barron D. Wilkins, an entrepreneur and local political figure. By the mid-1920s the gangsters had moved in on most of the more elegant and popular clubs, forcing the black owners to sell but sometimes allowing them to remain on the premises as managers or front men. Wilkins declined to sell and said so loudly and publicly in Harlem. One morning in 1926 he was

---

[16]Under Prohibition the manufacture and sale of beer with a drastically lowered alcoholic content was permitted. Derisively called "near beer" by devotees of the true brew, it could be spiked in various ways, including spraying it with ether.

knifed to death by a thug called Yellow Charleston, a dope addict and professional assassin.

Harlem also featured dozens of cafés, bars with music, hangout joints, and low dives, many of which Waller frequented or knew. Directly above Connie's Inn was the Performers and Entertainers Club, a small after-hours room where he sometimes played solo piano. The Rhythm Club was a jam session spot; the number of first-class musicians anxious to get on the bandstand was so large that they had to line up against a wall and wait their turn. It was here that Waller met Louis Armstrong in 1924 when the trumpeter came to New York to join Fletcher Henderson's band. At Tillie's Chicken Shack, lyricist Walter Donaldson, who wrote the words for *My Blue Heaven,* once offered Waller a free drink everytime he played the song. Tom obliged by playing it twenty-five times during the course of the evening.

Pod & Jerry's, Big John's Cafe, The Fat Man's Cafe, and Reuben's were all gathering places for musicians to eat, socialize, and jam. Among the low dives, Edmund's Cellar was, in the words of the great singer and actress Ethel Waters, "the last stop on the way down." Owned by Edmund "Mule" Brown, a former boxer, the dive sometimes featured "pansy parades," transvestite fashion shows, and lewd vaudeville. Walter "One Leg Shadow" Gould, one of the earliest of the stride pianists, was fired by Brown because the pianist couldn't read music to accompany singers.

Other establishments of note in Harlem included the boardinghouses on West 131st Street run by Mrs. Lottie Joplin, widow of ragtime king Scott Joplin, and Hazel Valentine's dicty whorehouse, the Daisy Chain. Among Mrs. Joplin's tenants was Ferdinand La Menthe "Jelly Roll" Morton, the first great jazz composer and a superb pianist, unfairly dismissed by Johnson, Waller, and Smith as old-fashioned. Hazel Valentine was a jolly bawd, much liked and respected by musicians. When James P. Johnson showed off his Cadillac automobile and invited some friends to take a spin to Mount Vernon, the party included Waller and Hazel, to whom Waller dedicated his piano solo *Valentine Stomp,* recorded in 1929. When the party returned from the outing, the car was seized by agents of the auto dealer— James P. hadn't kept up the payments.

Endemic to Harlem culture were the hundreds of churches and "sanctified tabernacles," many of them storefront operations maintained by various Baptist sects, and the dozens of zany religious cults presided over by foxy divines who convinced their eager believers that they were godly messengers masquerading as fleshly mortals. "Sweet Daddy" Grace was one of these messiahs; he concluded his harangues with a call for his congregation to "put some sugar on my table"—whereupon the sheep of his flock obligingly covered his table with dollar bills.

There were also social messiahs, thinkers, poets, and adventurers. The Jamaican Marcus Garvey founded a "back to Africa" movement and took subscriptions from his followers to purchase an ocean liner which would be the maiden ship of the "Black Star Line." He collected hundreds of thousands of dollars, finally got around to purchasing a floating hulk, and was sent to the Atlanta Penitentiary for fraud before any of his converts could drown themselves by setting sail on his leaky tub.

The black novelist Claude McKay wrote *Home to Harlem,* which enjoyed a brief vogue with the white and black intelligentsia. The poet Langston Hughes was fusing black speech rhythms with experiments in poetic meter. The philosopher W. E. B. Du Bois, frustrated over the social position and treatment of his race, turned to Marxism and its totalitarian solutions. "Colonel" Herbert Fauntleroy Julian, having barely learned to fly an airplane before announcing his intention to equal Charles Lindbergh (who flew from New York to Paris, nonstop, in 1927), invited all Harlem to see him take off for France. The crowds turned out, and the *Black Eagle* zoomed off the ground to wild hurrahs, flew for a few hundred feet, and plopped into the Harlem River—but no matter, his intentions for the race were good.

As black stage entertainments became more ambitious and their popularity increased, Waller was frequently called upon to provide material. In 1926 he and lyricist Spencer Williams contributed to *Tan Town Topics,* a hit revue presented at the Lafayette Theatre. One of Waller's songs from the score, *Senorita Mine,* was a national smash. In 1928 the comedy team of Miller and Lyles devised a script for a full-blown Broadway production, *Keep Shufflin',* and word went out that Harlem's best composers were wanted for the score. Waller and James P. Johnson, working with their own lyricists, provided much of the material. *Willow Tree,* by Waller and Andy Razaf, was a standout, but James P. had the hit of the show with '*Sippi.* Between the acts, the two pianists seated themselves at two concert grands for a special essaying of the tune which the program described: "On the white keys, Fats Waller—on the black keys, James P. Johnson—on the bugle, Jabbo Smith." A newspaper review of the show described the dual performances as virtuoso statements by "the two best left hands in the business."

Waller's growing career as a stage musical composer was interrupted by the longest of his jail sentences for alimony debts, but when he came out in 1929 Razaf had an assignment for him. Connie's Inn was presenting a new floor show, and tunes were required. Razaf lured Waller to his house in Asbury Park, where he had arranged a gargantuan buffet. There the two wrote and composed *My Fate Is in Your Hands* and *Zonky,* a piping hot number, in ninety minutes. Waller began to trace a third melody, to be used in the show as background music for soft-shoe dancing by the chorus. Razaf applied lyrics to the first statement, and Waller added a "bridge"—the middle eight bars of the tune—before suddenly announcing that he had "a heavy date" in New York and departing. Razaf continued to work on the third tune, but found that he couldn't remember the bridge. He called Waller's house; Anita referred him to another number. Finally locating Waller, Razaf explained that he'd forgotten the bridge. Tom replied that he'd forgotten the melody. Razaf hummed the main theme and then talked the lyrics to the middle eight bars. Waller hummed back a musical line for the bridge. Razaf excitedly told Waller to hang on and dashed to the piano, where he played the whole tune through, singing the lyrics. He jumped up and ran back to the telephone, joyfully proclaiming that the tune worked, then stopped talking when he heard the dial tone and realized that Waller had hung up some time before. The composition was *Ain't Misbehavin'.*

Load of Coal, as staged at Connie's, was a rousing success, and the team won the assignment for the score of the next show, to be titled *Hot Chocolates.* Three of Waller's most potent melodies were included: *Black and Blue, Sweet Savannah Sue,* and

Ain't Misbehavin'—Razaf remembered the last tune as being composed and written in forty minutes flat, allowing for telephone calls.

The process of musical creation is still little understood by scientists, psychiatrists, critics, and other embalmers. The process defies all attempts to probe the workings of its magic. It consists, at root, of talent, and the combustion of composing a melody involves an alchemy of heart, brains, and gizzard. Waller's method of composing was to place himself, or allow himself to be placed, in the most casual and/or convivial atmosphere possible, and then simply let the music roll out. Mary Lou Williams, an accomplished jazz pianist, saw Waller at Connie's Inn during an early rehearsal for *Hot Chocolates* and recalled this picture of the composer at work:

> The OAO [one and only] sat overflowing the piano stool, a jug of whiskey within easy reach. Leonard Harper, the producer, said, "Have you anything written for this number, Fats?" And Fats would reply, "Yeah, go on ahead with the dance, man." Then he composed his number while the girls were dancing. He must have composed the whole show . . . while I was sitting there—ears working overtime.
>
> Meanwhile, he bubbled over with so many stories and funny remarks that those girls could hardly hoof it for laughing. The girls, thirty-five to forty-dollar-a-week chorus beauties, were loaded with enough ice around their shapely ankles to sink a battleship, for these were generous days in New York.
>
> After the rehearsal one of the boys—knowing my memory—bet Fats I could repeat all the tunes he had just written, a bet Fats snapped up at paying odds.
>
> Falling apart with nerves at having to play before this big name, I was prodded to the piano but managed to concentrate and play nearly everything I had heard Fats play. He was knocked out, picking me up and throwing me in the air and roaring like a crazy man.

It was delightfully typical of Tom Waller that the grand gesture was the only kind he ever made.

Shortly after Waller composed *Hot Chocolates,* an article on him appeared in the *New York World-Telegram* in which his dealings with publishers was described:

> The high spot of Waller's career . . . took place at Carnegie Hall where he was the soloist at the recital of W. C. Handy's group of blues interpreters [April 27, 1928; Waller also performed James P. Johnson's piano rhapsody, *Yamekraw*]. Here he came into contact with white composers and publishers. He discovered that it was easy to sell tunes to white song-writers, who would vary them slightly and re-sell them as their own. The average rate for such a song, he says, was $250. Among the songs thus disposed of was one which knocked about for three seasons until it was finally inserted in a musical comedy. Featured in that show, it became the best seller of its season and netted $17,500 to its "composer," who paid "Fatts" [*sic*] $500 for it.

Ten years later a perturbed reader of *Variety,* the show business newspaper, wrote a letter complaining about a Waller radio broadcast:

> First of all Waller was especially entertaining and began to take on solos with his usual [comic] remarks. Then the remarks became unusual, running something like this: "Wonder what the po' people's doin', music publishers got plenty"; then later, "Music publishers won't send you free music 'less you gonna broadcast it." The announcer made a couple of remarks sounding pretty embarrassed, "Let's stick to singing," and then closed the program at the half-hour with, "Now it's time to say goodbye to Fats Waller and his music . . . and even if it weren't time, it would be a good idea."

The writer, one J. Gordon Thornton, closed his letter by asking: "Will you tell me what Waller's grievance is?" *Variety* could not very well reply without opening a discussion of trade secrets.

10
Radio Papa, Broadcastin' Mama

THE GREAT DEPRESSION, which began with the Wall Street "Black Thursday" panic of September 28, 1929, was the most terrible and extended economic disaster in the history of the United States. Its effects were so cataclysmic that an entire generation of Americans bore emotional scars from it.

Thousands of corporations, large and small, declared bankruptcy and closed their doors. Millions of people were out of work. Evicted from their homes, apartments, and farms, they slept in public parks and migrated about the country in rattletrap cars or clung to the underbars of freight trains, hoping to find jobs somewhere. Even the banks collapsed. In New York a particular corner of a tall office building became known as "Millionaire's Leap" from the number of suicides who used it as a jumping-off point.

Though the full effects of the stock market crash did not filter down to business, workers, and communities until 1930, and though the nadir of the Great Depression did not come until 1931-1932, the Depression's effects on the small and loosely organized recording industry were more immediate. Most of the labels which regularly recorded jazz did so for a black audience with limited disposable income. Soon after the Depression struck, most of these labels found that their audience had evaporated. Victor Records, which had only partially invested in jazz recording, managed to hang on, but its nearest rival, Columbia Records, declared bankruptcy, while small labels like Gennett, Paramount, and Perfect disappeared.

Waller was hurt by the Depression, for quick money from recording sessions was one of his major sources of income. In 1929 he appeared on more than twenty titles; in 1930 he appeared on only one. Victor thought it would be interesting to have an "old-style" and modern pianist play the same selection and then issue their versions back to back. Jelly Roll Morton was cast for the former role and Waller for the latter, but Morton—who was very touchy—did not show up for the date, so Waller and another pianist, Bennie Paine, who was called in at the last minute, played a duet of *St. Louis Blues*.

Had Waller remained in New York throughout the worst years of the Depression, with the record and band business taking such thumps, he would have been in trouble. But he had angel's luck that turned the economic and social horrors of the Depression into a major boost for his career.

What happened to Waller was, in a word, radio.

Little more than a toy, and a crude one at that, in the early 1920s, by the end of the decade the medium had grown in technical power and skill of program presentation. Wattage increased; signals were cleaner, clearer, and stronger. The medium was beginning to attract some of the biggest stars in the entertainment world, among them Paul Whiteman's orchestra, then the leading band in the country.[17] Until the very early 1930s,

---

[17]As much as radio helped Waller's career, it had the reverse effect on Bix Beiderbecke's. As the Whiteman band appeared more frequently on radio, there were new tunes to learn every week by sight-reading. Bix, who was not a facile reader, became more baffled and frustrated and increased his drinking to the point where Whiteman had to send him home to Iowa, for a cure—at full pay. Bix hoped to rejoin the band, but Roy Bargy, a pianist and adviser to Whiteman, vetoed Bix's return, as the orchestra was concentrating more and more on radio as a vehicle. The Depression forced Whiteman to cut Bix's sick-leave salary to half-pay and then to terminate it. Bix came back to New York in 1930, went off the cure, played a few radio and record dates with pickup bands, and died of pneumonia in August 1931.

there were few dramatic programs or "acted" series; most of what radio offered was music. When the Depression reached nadir, radio was the one means the average person had to escape the awful realities of life. Records were too expensive, and there were few operating labels left. Even the dime admission to a double-feature movie was often more than a family could afford. But radio was free. It was a comfort and a pleasure, and the battered, frightened nation came to depend on it.

Waller was not a stranger to radio; his first broadcast was from the stage of the Fox Terminal Theatre in Newark, New Jersey, in 1923, where he played with Clarence Williams' Blue Five group. Waller's unofficial manager, "Captain" George Maines, later placed him on various local programs beamed from stations WHN and WOR in 1928-1929. These were one- or two-shot appearances.

But in December 1930, after Waller deputized for his friend Jesse Crawford, playing the massive organ at the Paramount Theatre on Broadway and West Forty-fourth Street, the Paramount Company decided to book Waller on its new radio program, "Paramount on Parade." Originally scheduled for thirteen weeks, the program caught on so well that its run was extended to twenty-six weeks, winding up in June 1931. Waller went straight into another air show, "Radio Roundup," playing, singing, and inserting his sassy jibes at the lyrics. Waller's principal publisher at the time was Joe Davis, to whom Waller was nominally under contract. What the "contract" broke down to was Davis' having first chance at all new Waller material, plus occasional cash advances, plus a weekly stipend and Waller's presence in the office between ten and five to provide piano accompaniments to singers demonstrating new material. Davis advised Waller to do as much singing as possible on the radio programs, since he wanted to advance Waller's value as an entertainer (and, simultaneously, as a plugger of Davis-owned material).

Because of Waller's popularity on the two radio shows, Davis was able to convince bandleader Ted Lewis to use Tom on a 1931 session which also included Benny Goodman, then a freelance musician; cornetist Muggsy Spanier; and George Brunies, the original trombonist for the great New Orleans Rhythm

Kings. One of the titles was Waller's *Crazy 'bout My Baby*. Shortly after the Lewis session, made for tottering Columbia Records, the label recorded him as a solo performer, with Waller again essaying *Crazy 'bout My Baby*. But where he had sung and played "straight" on the Lewis date, Waller let his frisky nature take over on the solo session. It is the first example of what was to be, in many ways, the standard Waller recorded performance for the rest of his life; in it he used the technique of communicating with an unseen audience which he had learned in a year of radio work.

The recording opens with a spoken mixture of *Commedia del'arte* and genial buffoonery:

> My *goodness,* I feel so effervescent this mornin'. . . . *mmmmmmh!* The feelin' is *so* eulogizin'. . . . Listen, can ya stand me to tell ya 'bout it? Listen here—

He sings the tune through and then takes a first piano chorus, inserting:

> Let's go uptown. . . . Boy, will you git off? . . . Now we're floatin' up the Hudson. . . . awww, mercy, you slay me, you sweet thing—*mmmmh!*

Waller sings the bridge again, takes a second piano chorus, sings the last verse, and closes with daffy comments as he plays a chain of chords:

> I'm exasperated by my offspring—my offspring is exasperatin' me. . . . Listen, baby, would you like to come over for a cup of coffee—*mmmmh*—baby! maybe!

The record contained all the hallmarks of Waller's stardom, which would not come for another three years: the superb pianistics, the vocal horseplay, and the feeling that he was unabashedly enjoying himself. The third factor is what made him famous and loved. Few performers of his time could strike an immediate comradeship with their audiences and become so intimate while retaining the artistic distance necessary to perform.

It may seem ironic that with the hundreds of titles Tom Waller recorded between 1922 and 1931 he was not well known outside New York, and it is perhaps difficult for the contemporary generation, which believes that record labels have the power to make or break artists and that record labels determine what is played on the radio,[18] to realize that labels in the 1920s and 1930s had very little to do with establishing performers as major recording artists, nor did they make much effort to do so.

In those decades a recording star was considered an act of God by record labels. Whatever promotional efforts were made by labels were made after the fact; there was no conception of "building" a performer exclusively via records. Labels looked for hit songs, not performers who were able to sustain themselves, with the result that the labels were almost totally dependent on music publishers to provide the songs, and often left the choice of performers up to music publishers and their "song-plugger" agents.

It was a rare performer who sold a million copies[19] of a record. The Original Dixieland Jazz Band did so in 1917 with the first issued jazz record, *Livery Stable Blues;* singer Gene Austin struck fire with *My Blue Heaven* in 1924; Mamie Smith's 1923 *Crazy Blues* was a gigantic hit; and the vaudevillian Cliff "Ukulele Ike" Edwards, a combination of minstrel and Dutch uncle, had two best sellers with *June Night* and *I Cried for You.* But none of these artists were groomed by labels; they were accidental stars. The Original Dixieland Jazz Band happened to be the

---

[18]Neither belief is true, nor has it ever been true.

[19]All "million-selling" claims prior to 1960 are suspect or cannot be verified. It was not until that year that the Recording Industry Association of America required its member labels to submit documented proof of record sales so that an official RIAA certificate could be issued. The ruling was made because of the number of suspicious "gold record" awards made by labels to artists for purposes of ballyhooing a record or the label itself, or as a public relations effort to keep a recording artist happy. The first "official" presentation of a "gold record" was made by RCA Victor in the early 1940s to Glenn Miller & His Orchestra for their recording of *Chattanooga Choo Choo.* The presentation took place during a "remote" radio broadcast from a hotel where Miller was appearing. Needless to say, the "remote" was beamed from a station owned by RCA.

first jazz group to record; as recording artists, they were finished by 1922. Austin continued to be successful because he represented the ultimate in the boy-crooner vocal type of the time, and because he was a skilled performer who relied equally on sentimentality and his careful, knowledgeable phrasing of a lyric line. Mamie Smith's record proved that there was a previously unexplored and considerable market of black record buyers, but her fame was fleeting. Edwards was already a star in vaudeville with enormous public exposure; his career was crippled by the death of his label, Perfect, soon after the Depression struck and by the demise of vaudeville, which was replaced first by movies and then by radio.

So it is not surprising that Tom Waller should have recorded so prolifically for ten years but never become known outside New York and points north. He had appeared on small band sides; as soloist with orchestras, such as Fletcher Henderson and McKinney's Cotton Pickers; with small groups such as Morris' Hot Babies; and as a piano and organ soloist under his own name. Nearly all of his hundreds of recordings were made for Victor, yet there was never an effort on Victor's part, though it was well acquainted with his talent and versatility, to push him as an artist except to the black market, and even within that limited sphere it did not push hard. He received less attention than did Jelly Roll Morton's Red Hot Peppers, who were billed by the label as "Victor's #1 Hot Band," but only because their issued records sold well.

The modern concept of a label's being intimately involved in building the career of a recording artist because of his or her commercial or prestige value was largely unknown during the 1920s and 1930s. Labels considered their functions to be that of the laboratory (the technical quality of the recording) and the vendor (placing the goods on the market). Labels thought small, and often acted small.

So it is not surprising that Waller's 1931 solo version of *Crazy 'bout My Baby* did not sell more than moderately, given the label promotion of the time—the era of "Throw it at the wall, and if it sticks it's a hit."

Being a free-lancer, and hurting from the drying up of record-

The ebullient Fats Waller at a radio broadcast in the 1930s. The man leaning on the piano is Paul Douglas, who began his career as a radio announcer and later became a well-known actor in films, especially for his role co-starring with Judy Holliday in *The Solid Gold Cadillac*. *Photograph from Photo Files*

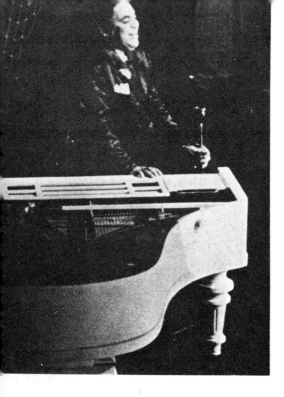

Waller takes a curtain call after a performance at the London Palladium in 1938. His appearance in England was an enormous success and established him as an international artist. He returned the following year and also toured Scandinavia. *Photograph from Photo Files*

A rare shot of Waller with his first manager, Phil Ponce. It was Ponce who made the two moves that in large part determined Waller's stardom. The first was in 1932, when he secured Waller a year's contract with a radio station WLW in Cincinnati, whose powerful signal gained Waller a huge Midwestern audience; the second came in 1934 when Ponce signed him with Victor Records as an exclusive artist. But Waller was an exasperating client, and by 1938 Ponce, who was old and ill, asked Ed Kirkeby to take over.

Photograph from ASCAP

A Mona Lisa look: this candid portrait captures the often baffling elements of both child and man in Waller's extraordinary personality.
Photograph from ASCAP

Fats giving the "sent" eyeball roll at a dance date in Denver in 1941.
Photograph from Photo Files

A somewhat mysterious shot. The dreamy look may mean that Waller is thinking of what he is going to play with his right hand while his left hand is working out the bass line on a melody. While the exact date and place of this photo are unknown, it is from late in his life, possibly at a 1941 solo piano session or the "V-disk" session of 1943, his last record date.

Photograph from Photo Files

Waller and the Rhythm at a 1941 recording date in Victor's Chicago studios. Fats is at the organ and in easy reach of the piano; he played both instruments on a number of tunes. The Rhythm, from left to right: Eugene "Honey Bear" Sedric, John "Bugs" Hamilton, Al Casey (partially obscured by microphone), "Slick" Jones, and Cedric Wallace.

Photograph from Photo Files

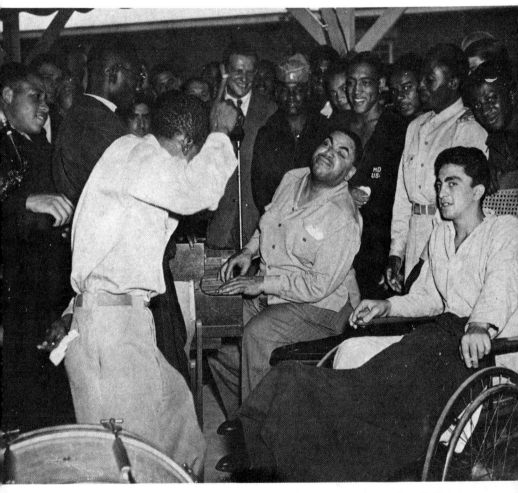

A performance for veterans of the 1942-43 North African campaign. Waller's insistence on playing benefits for servicemen during World War II (he never refused a request and often volunteered) may have contributed to his failing health and early death.

Photograph from Culver Pictures

Playing his favorite instrument—the organ—Waller excelled in his treatment of spirituals, which invoked the memory of his mother. *Photograph from the Bettmann Archive*

The quintessential Waller: a derby hat, a jug of gin, and wow! This picture was originally a publicity still used by Twentieth Century-Fox studios to promote Waller's appearance in the 1943 film, *Stormy Weather.*   Photograph from Culver Pictures

ing dates, Waller looked for other sources of income after the "Radio Roundup" program ended in 1932. Finding none, and always ready to abandon business for pleasure, he looked for new adventure.

John Hammond, the eminent jazz entrepreneur-historian-discologist, remembers "going to Fats' twenty-eighth birthday party. He was living on 135th Street with Anita. Fats and the brilliant Reginald Forsythe were at the piano, playing *Petrushka* with four hands."

Forsythe, who composed *Serenade for a Wealthy Widow* (Waller recorded it in 1934 and included his famous wisecrack, "Woman, I hear you're flooded with currency!") was one of the small group of black musicians and songwriters who emigrated to England and France during the 1920s seeking relief from career frustrations and the American racial attitude of the time.

Another expatriate was Waller's old friend and collaborator Spencer Williams, who provided the laundered lyrics to *Squeeze Me* in 1925. Williams was living in France and came to the United States for a visit. Finding himself short of money, he enthusiastically described Paris to Waller, who determined that he must see the city. After Waller sweet-talked Anita into permitting him to go, he and Williams turned out twenty-seven melodies in three days (the figure is also given as one hundred) and made a quick sale to publishers. Waller and Williams booked passage on the luxury liner *Île de France* for its July 1932 sailing.

After an all-night party celebrating their coming adventure, the two musicians boarded the liner to begin a five-day cruise which the passengers and crew would have cause to remember. The irrepressible Waller sped to the piano in the ship's lounge whenever possible, and his rowdy camaraderie delighted all. He also drank deep of the ship's liquor supply.

Once arrived in Paris, Waller found several things to delight him. The first was the fable of the city and its powerful charm— considerably purer in 1932 than it is today. Waller was, in the title of George Gershwin's famous suite, an American in Paris. There was also the absence of the color line; wherever Waller went, he was treated as an equal. Parisians at that time were refreshingly free of racism, as were Londoners. In 1932 London and Paris were the capitals of great colonial empires, and the citizens of both England and France were used to exotic specimens and rather fond of them. Forty years later the English and French, with millions of former colonial peoples swarming into their capitals, and with their empires gone, would not be so welcoming and would discover that they, like the United States, had a race problem. But in 1932 life for a black expatriate or a black visitor was sweet.

There was another factor: the Great Depression, begun in America, had not reached Europe with full force, and France in 1932 was relatively untouched by what was soon to become the world economic crisis. Therefore, what money Waller and Williams brought over—at the prevailing exchange rate—was " righteous gold"; American dollars converted into French francs (the franc having been an anemic currency for several years) went farther and bought more. Waller and Williams found plenty of opportunities for spending as they made the rounds of cafés and clubs in the Rue Pigalle area.

"Waiter, bring me a dozen of them mam'selles!" Waller roared in a café. Allowing a moment for his words to be translated, there followed hearty laughs and cheers from the customers. Waller got his mam'selles, and his wine and champagne, and was always quick to seat himself at the piano and treat the amazed and delighted Gauls to generous chunks of his "stride" style.

While in Paris, Waller made several convivial appearances at Bricktop's, a club owned by a black American woman who was cashing in on the French fascination for things negro, typified by their adoration of Josephine Baker, a former Harlem dancer who had removed to France and gotten up a modified striptease in a club program called the *Revue Nègre*.

Waller also claimed to have been invited to the Notre Dame Cathedral by a French admirer to try its massive and superb organ, and is supposed to have enjoyed a rare moment testing the Notre Dame "God-box."

During his Paris stay, Waller moved about various clubs, but he seems to have settled on a bistro called La Rumba as his unofficial home base. Here he met the French jazz enthusiast and critic Hughes Panassié, who had been chasing him around various cafés, knowing that Waller was in town but not knowing precisely where. On meeting the round brown man, Panassié was given a letter of introduction from John Hammond, although this was hardly necessary since Panassié was already a Waller fan from hearing his records. He asked Waller to play *Sweet Savannah Sue* and was surprised and somewhat distressed when Waller confessed that he couldn't remember the tune. Panassié was unaware that his hero had been composing melodies almost instantaneously and under great pressure for "fast gold" for nearly a decade, with the result that tunes sometimes left Waller as rapidly as they came to him. But Panassié was quick to see, with awe, that the pianist had a miraculous capacity for drink—the French, whatever their political imbecilities, had not sunk so low as to impose such a law as Prohibition—and he also observed that

> . . . far from forgetting music when he stopped playing, he loved it so much that he lived it every instant. While . . . talking to me with one ear, he continued to listen to what [the house band] was playing behind him, so that any given moment he might break off in the middle of a sentence, exclaim, "What a pretty piece that is!," get up, go . . . and find out the title, and then come back and tell me as he sat down again.

But the good times had to end when the money ran out, as it did. Waller's and Williams' original plans for their visit are somewhat in doubt. Waller told Panassié that he was not booked for any professional performances—that is, he was on vacation—but also said that he expected to go to London and appear at a club. The circumstances of Waller's departure are also in some doubt. According to Williams, Waller played a trick on him by wiggling his eyebrows at a mam'selle leaving La Rumba, and then sending the girl back to tell Williams that Waller was departing. Williams is then supposed to have rushed to their hotel, only to find Waller gone, headed for Le Havre and a boat that was soon leaving for New York. An explanation given of the incident is that Waller's famed homesickness for

Harlem was too much to bear, and Tom is supposed to have wired an acquaintance who worked in Irving Berlin's music publishing office to cable him the money for return fare. Yet John Hammond wrote at the time that he was "distressed to learn that [Waller] did not get to England because of some consular difficulty," meaning that Tom, being black, had run afoul of the white American foreign service.

Whatever the reason, Waller came back to New York and regaled his Harlem constituency with tales of his adventures in Paris. He also appeared on two recording sessions in those parched days for recording dates, one with Jack Teagarden's dance/jazz orchestra, where he and Mr. T indulged in some wonderful vocal banter, and the other a red-hot, boiling session with a pickup group, including rock-solid drummer Zutty Singleton, searing clarinetist/saxophonist Pee Wee Russell, and the pugnacious banjo of wheeler-dealer Eddie Condon, who'd gotten Tom to the 1929 *Harlem Fuss/Minor Drag* session on time. Vaudevillian and café owner Billy Banks supplied the vocals, straining his boy-tenor to the limit to keep up with the frenzy generated on *I Would Do Anything for You, Mean Old Bed Bug Blues, Yellow Dog Blues,* and *Yes Suh!* All present at the sessions were sufficiently lubricated to be relaxed and fanciful, but there is a desperation underlying the performances which shows just how tight things were for jazz musicians during the Depression; jazz dates were few, money was scarce, and the panic was on.

But by the end of that year Waller's angel's luck came through again. He took on a full-time manager, Phil Ponce, who got him a one-shot appearance over radio station WLW in Cincinnati, Ohio, then as now one of the most powerful transmitters in the Midwest. Waller's initial appearance was successful enough for Ponce to secure a two-year contract, and a program was devised called "Fats Waller's Rhythm Club." The format consisted of a "deacon" hearing the woes of a member of his flock who confessed that he was infected by jazz—Waller could not have failed to notice the accidental similarities of the plot to his own relationship with his God-bawling father—and the program always ended with the "deacon" succumbing to the syncopated virus.

The show was an immediate hit, and for the first time in his professional life Waller became a regional celebrity instead of a local hero. His performances and personality won and kept a Midwest audience of thousands for him, and the success of his program, touted by manager Ponce, would be noted by New York radio executives two years later.

Despite his yearning for Harlem—which later often caused him to skedaddle in the midst of road tours and earned him a bad name with promoters and bookers—Waller spent more than a year in the Midwest, his longest sustained absence from New York, and he made no recordings in 1933. He was earning steady money at WLW, and the Depression was gutting the music market in New York, with hundreds of excellent musicians frantically trying to land what few jobs were available. Another incentive to stay in the Midwest was to avoid process servers and other legal grief stemming from his on-again, off-again alimony payments. All things considered, he was better off in the provinces.

Waller also appeared, unannounced, on a late-night mood-music program titled "Moon River," which featured romantic and light classical selections performed on the organ. He was happy to play, since he loved both the instrument and the material, and he accepted the station's explanation that it couldn't identify him because the audience might be perplexed that he could be so rowdy and rascally on the "Rhythm Club" and yet so delicate a few hours later. It was a relaxing and inspiring nightly assignment for Waller, though the station management personnel were annoyed that he used the loft of the Wurlitzer as a wastebasket for his empty gin bottles.

Shortly after the "Rhythm Club" program began, Waller was advised that a pretty young pianist from Xenia, Ohio, who played somewhat in his style, might be a neat addition to the cast. Waller sent for Una Mae Carlisle, who was then in her mid-teens, to come to Cincinnati. When she got to the studio she sat at the piano to practice and, looking up, saw Waller making silly faces at her through the glass panel of the engineer's booth. She debuted on the "Rhythm Club" that evening, during the Christmas week of 1932. So began a sometimes vexing, sometimes hilarious relationship. Though they respected each other as musicians they quarreled frequently over Waller's zany ways.

When the RKO booking office decided to send the "Rhythm" cast on a theatrical tour, the skirmishes between Waller and Carlisle increased with the pressures of the road—something Tom was used to but which irritated the inexperienced girl. When the tour reached Youngstown, Ohio, a depressing steel town, the manager of the show skipped out with all the money that had been collected. A cousin of Una Mae's helped the band straggle back to Cincinnati. A few months later they were offered a date at a Louisville, Kentucky, country club. Having resumed the radio program, the cast had a little money between them, so they all chipped in to buy a car in which, Waller announced, they would drive down to Louisville in style. Una Mae was told to be set for departure early in the morning. At six-thirty she was ready. No Waller. Noon came, and still no Waller, so she caught a train to Louisville and, knowing his tastes, phoned the best hotel in town and discovered that he had registered that morning. She made for the hotel, and as she arrived a taxi whirled around the corner, bearing the pianist, the cast member who played the deacon, and two giggly ladies. The outraged Carlisle stepped into the street and halted the cab, then advanced on it while giving Waller hell. The pianist got out of the car and warily backed away from Una Mae, offering soothing words and plentiful excuses to "Sister Gizzard-Lip."

Waller's Cincinnati sojourn ended in early 1934. He returned to New York without a steady job and with no immediate prospects, but he filled in at various Harlem clubs and at Adrian's Tap Room, a cafe and music showcase in the Broadway theater district owned by the now little remembered but highly accomplished Adrian Rollini, who "invented" the bass saxophone as a jazz instrument in the 1920s and whose exciting use of it made an impression on young Coleman Hawkins, then a member of Fletcher Henderson's reed section. It was in 1934 that Henderson's great band broke up. "Smack" had been seriously injured in a car accident and was in constant pain as well as a state of depression. Although economic circumstances had hurt his orchestra, its members, loyal to him and to the spirit of the band, continued to play dates even though they were sometimes not paid for their services. No one in the band wanted to be the first to leave, so they resigned en masse.

Though Waller could usually manage to pick up eating money by guesting at the keyboard, economic circumstances in New York, combined with the lack of radio work and recording sessions, made him feel the pinch. In many ways it was as though he were twenty years old again, just starting off and taking what jobs he could find. He seemed to have come full circle. There was even a call to entertain at a Park Avenue party with Willie "The Lion" Smith, as they had done in the old days. Waller accepted.

He and Smith were tapped by maestro Paul Whiteman, who was in charge of providing the musical entertainment for a Park Avenue revel celebrating George Gershwin's birthday. To Waller it must have seemed like old home week. Gershwin, internationally famous, had been the unofficial student of James P. Johnson, Smith, and Waller, while Waller had later studied classical piano with Gershwin's brother-in-law, Leopold Godowski.

While the guests chattered and Gershwin moved among his well-wishers, Waller dived into his act, playing, singing, and mugging. Soon, as always, he had a squad of people gathered around the piano watching him work. One of them was a teenage girl who seemed especially delighted. She ran over to her father and pointed Waller out. After the pianist finished his set, the man came over and gave him a phone number. The man was William S. Paley, head of the Columbia Broadcasting System. The next day Waller phoned, and later that day Paley issued orders that a program on the network's schedule was to be found for Waller.

By the middle of the year Thomas Waller would be a star.

11
That Rhythm Man

ALL THE ELEMENTS to catalyze Waller's career into a burst of happy glory were present in the spring of 1934. William S. Paley's imprimatur brought Waller guest shots on several CBS programs; by early summer Waller had his own "Rhythm Club" broadcasts on Monday and Thursday nights, plus an organ program on Saturday nights and alternate Sunday evening appearances on the "Columbia Variety Hour." In that same spring the energetic Phil Ponce went to Victor and worked out an exclusive recording contract for Waller with a royalty rate of three percent and a cash advance of $100 for each recording session. The debut date of Fats Waller & His Rhythm took place in May. Fittingly, the first tune recorded was *A Porter's Love Song to a Chambermaid,* composed by James P. Johnson with exceptionally bright and witty lyrics by Andy Razaf:

> I am the happiest of troubadours—
> Thinkin' of you, baby, while I'm massaging those floors—
> In my leisure time
> I've made up this rhyme:

93

I will be your oil mop
If you'll be the oil;
Then we both could mingle
Every time we toil.

I will be the washboard
If you'll be the tub;
Think of all the Mondays
We could rub-a-dub.
. . . .
I will be your window
If you'll be my shade:
That's a porter's love song
To a chambermaid.

A second session in August yielded the charming *Have a Little Dream on Me;* then in September came Reginald Forsythe's
Serenade for a Wealthy Widow, a miniconcerto masquerading as
a pop tune, plus a riotous version of Irving Berlin's shy proposal
of marriage, *Mandy (There's a Minister Handy),* where the
Rhythm's performance turns the imagined wedding into a cheerfully pagan affair, with trumpeter Herman Autry taking a torch-
hot chorus with a growl mute in the bell of his horn; and as
Waller goes into his piano solo, he roars: "*Awwwwww,* the ticklin's *so* terrific—*stop* it now!"

Two November dates brought a version of *Honeysuckle Rose,*
the delightful *Breakin' the Ice* and *Dream Man,* with Waller
inventing a minidrama about the sleeper being awakened by the
landlady pounding on his door as a prelude to a demand for
back rent. The second November date was a solo piano session,
Waller's first in five years: *African Ripples* was an extension of
an idea Waller first used on *Gladyse,* a 1929 solo, while *Viper's
Drag,* a tone poem on marijuana[20] reflects the alternate calm

---

[20]*Viper* was a 1920s/1930s term for a pot smoker; the pot was known as
"tea" and the marijuana cigarette as a "muggle." Louis Armstrong described
his experiences with marijuana in *Satchmo,* by Max Jones and John Chilton,
and in a 1932 recording of *I'll Be Glad When You're Dead, You Rascal You,*
Armstrong interpolated the lines, "I'll be standin' on the corner high/When
they bring your body by." Judging from his guffaws and goofy behavior, he
may have been under the influence on the date.

and giddiness experienced with a smoke. Waller divides the two sensations, portraying the initial calm by inserting phrases from the "In the Hall of the Mountain King" subsection of Grieg's *Peer Gynt Suite,* and then demonstrating the litmus of the muggle-giggles by a surge of boiling-hot stride.

The constant exposure of Waller over the radio helped his record sales—again, it was a case of a label dealing with a pre-sold artist—but Victor was surprised at the response to the Waller series; otherwise, he would not have had five sessions in less than a year. Like most "overnight smashes," Waller became a national figure partly because he was unique, partly because of his experience, and partly because he was the right man at the right time. Though the nation was not as frightened and bewildered by the Depression as it had been five years previously, the economic situation and its attendant social disarray were still ugly facts of life, but sassy Tom Waller radiated heigh-ho confidence, and he was a champion at making people laugh and persuading them to dream. It was no accident that the three most popular personalities on radio during the 1930s were Freeman Gosden and Charles Correll, two white men who portrayed black fictional characters on the "Amos 'n' Andy" comedy program, and President Franklin D. Roosevelt, whose "fireside chats" were designed to lift the citizens' morale. Waller fell somewhere between them, but he fell in exactly the right place.

Another key to the success of the Rhythm records series was that it presented Waller with enough of a band behind him but not too much of a band to slow him down; the versatile combo was streamlined, full of zip and dash, sometimes a little rough around the edges, but adaptable to the various kinds of songs it was assigned to perform.

The personnel of the Rhythm remained fairly constant between 1934 and 1942. Guitarist Al Casey was a teenager going to Waller's alma mater, DeWitt Clinton High School in the Bronx, when he was picked for the group. Casey's uncles and aunt were the Southern Suns, who had appeared with Waller on his WLW program. Saxophonist/clarinetist Eugene "Honeybear" Sedric was spotted during a Waller tour of Harlem clubs where Waller dropped in to listen to various bands and combos, looking for recruits. Sedric had been active since 1924, when he came from St. Louis with Jimmy Cooper's Black & White Revue to play Hurtig & Seamon's Theatre before it was bought by Frank Schiffman and renamed the Apollo, and he had been to Europe with Sam Wooding's Orchestra in 1925. He was given his nickname for his resemblance in torso to Winnie-the-Pooh, and during stage shows Waller used to urge him on by yelling, "Git up on yo' feet, Baby Bear, and earn yo' salary!" Both Casey and Sedric became well known and respected through their association with Waller, and later fronted groups of their own.

The Rhythm was certainly one of the most productive combos that ever existed; it was not unusual for it to polish off as many as thirteen sides during a single recording session. The volume of quality performances becomes even more remarkable when it is noted that nearly all the selections on any given recording date were unfamiliar to the band. The material was picked by the Victor A & R (Artists & Repertoire) man, who was often guided by song pluggers peddling whatever their publisher employers wanted hawked. Waller would run through the tunes briefly at the piano while the Rhythm members familiarized themselves with the material; then a "head" arrangement was concocted and the recording session began. Waller usually submitted gracefully to the material presented to him, but there were times when he argued with A & R men over a particular selection which he felt was especially stupid or uninspired. Waller always lost the arguments, since the A & R man's word was law.[21] Waller's method of defense was to savage the dopey lyrics with sometimes abrasive buffoonery, and when Waller overacted on a tune it was a sure sign he didn't like it. But by and large, the quality of the material Waller recorded was no better or worse than that essayed by any major performer of the time: even those performers or entrepreneurs who had sustaining careers (vocalists Bing Crosby and Frank Sinatra, bandleaders Benny Goodman and Paul Whiteman) recorded their fair share of junk.

---

[21]The situation with major recording artists has been entirely reversed today. The A & R man's functions have been taken over by the producer, and the artist's will—or whim—is supreme.

Having been a commercial songwriter for ten years before his stardom, Waller was well aware of the pressures that sometimes led to the writing of throwaway tunes, and his own catalog contained a percentage, albeit a small percentage, of lackluster material. Normally a melodist, Waller wrote in phrases or riffs when he was hard pressed, or concocted hurried variations on well-known tunes. His *Jungle Jamboree,* recorded in 1929 by Duke Ellington's orchestra, owes the resolution of the tune to *Sweet Georgia Brown.*

It has been remarked by Waller fans, scholars, and partisans that his Rhythm series contains a burdensome amount of poor songs, the implication being that had Waller been allowed to choose his material or provide his own songs for recording sessions, he might have left a more "prestigious" legacy between 1934 and 1943. Realities argue against such a belief. Prior to 1934 Waller composed for a living as well as for musical expression and personal exuberance. As a free-lancer, he had lived from occasional paycheck to occasional paycheck; he was dependent on "fast gold." Once he became a recording star, steady money started coming in even faster than he could spend it; for the first time in his life he lived in financial security. Subtracting the considerable amounts of dough he spent on personal entertainment—food, drink, and companionship, all of which he consumed in enormous amounts—he was able, by 1935, to outfit himself and his family with first-class wardrobes and also to order a custom-built $7,200 Lincoln limousine and to maintain one of his many "cousins" as a chauffeur.

Once secure financially, his productivity as a composer declined—although his talent did not. His recorded performances, which nearly always included a vocal, were determined by his professional attitude toward a tune, and he kept in constant touch with Tin Pan Alley (the nickname for the songwriting industry of the day).

Joey Nash, first a saxophonist and later a radio crooner, provides a charming and incisive view into Waller's constant combination of the sensual and common sense in music. Nash met Waller on a train coming back to New York from Washington:

I had just finished a college gig with the Vincent Lopez band . . .
I hated the music business and fervently wished I was a ditch-
digger. My crumpled tuxedo, starched dress shirt and collar felt
grafted to my sweaty skin.

A laughing voice alongside of me said, "You have to admit you
can't beat the happy times and jolly moments a musician's life
has to offer, can you?" I wearily turned and gazed at an inflated
belly, big pop eyes, moustache, and a devastating smile. That was
my introduction to Fats Waller.

Though never quite a Waller protégé, Nash was the occasional
beneficiary of Waller's generous comradeship. Around 1935,
when Nash was singing on the "Studebaker Hour" radio program over CBS, Waller ran into him and praised his vocalizing.
The two then set out on a tour of Tin Pan Alley, where Waller
would sample and test the current product coming out of the
ditty factories of music publishers while his limousine circled
around West Forty-ninth and Fiftieth streets where the Brill
Building, home of Tin Pan Alley, was located. Nash and Waller
meandered from office to office, picking up sheet music as they
went along, until they arrived at a small rehearsal room with a
spinet or piano. Then the work session began:

"Sing this one, let's see how the lyric complements the tune,"
he'd say. . . . Playing for a singer, Fats said again and again, was
not appreciated by laymen and was a true test of a pianist's musical intelligence.

As a professional melodist long involved in the music industry, Waller wanted to see what the competition was doing and to
keep up-to-date with current trends, and he was always eager to
slip in one of his new tunes for recording sessions, such as *How
Can You Face Me?*, which Nash sang over the radio and which
the Rhythm recorded in its September 1934 session. The tune is
an unusually pedantic effort from Waller and his chief lyricist,
Andy Razaf.

Despite his being required to record tunes not of his choosing,
and despite the emphasis on upbeat novelty concoctions, Waller
lived and worked in the golden age of pop ballads and wise-

cracker courtship songs. The decades of the 1920s and 1930s
were, arguably, the most productive period of distinguished and
persuasive urban, literate popular music. The 1930s were a beneficiary of the adventurous and experimental music of the preced-
ing decade, when pop music began to absorb and adapt jazz,
classical, and futuristic elements, much as the Beatles personified
the high-water mark of the 1960s rock by their alchemy of styles
and their personal brilliance. The difference between the best of
the pop music of the 1930s, as opposed to that of the 1920s, was
that the later decade kept the essence of the new elements but
eliminated the silliness of the "Jazz Age" and "flaming youth."
The Depression replaced the sometimes arrogant innocence of
youth with quickly—and bitterly—acquired experience, and although tunes continued to be romantic and frisky, their descriptions of love or pleasure were definitions of adult behavior instead of candycane sentiments. In the Depression era, there
wasn't time to be cute or silly, and the fact of youth had no
social premium or mystique, as it does today. In the Depression,
people grew up fast or they died. Romance flourished, as it
always has and always will, but there was a pragmatic sense
about it: boy and girl, having met, had to face a confused and
hard world, and the successful spirit of their individuality and
their love had to be measured against reality. The facts of life
produced some remarkable and cherishable songs in the 1930s;
Waller sang some of them, including the Billy Rose tune *Have a
Little Dream on Me:*

> How'd'ja like a mansion in Manhattan,
> And a cozy cottage by the sea,
> How'd'ja like to dress in silk and satin?
> Baby, have a little dream on me.
> . . . .
> Paris in the spring, Miami in the fall,
> Interviews and pictures in the press;
> What a way to streak—on twenty bucks a week—
> Don't forget the Rockefellers started out with less.
>
> Everything we touch will turn to clover
> In the lovely land of what's to be;
> But until your baby puts it over,
> Baby, have a little dream on me.

Though Waller's vocals became increasingly raffish and his spoken asides zanier in the late 1930s as he grew impatient with low-grade material, the Rhythm sessions of 1934 and 1935 demonstrate that he could and would treat a respectable tune gently or do his utmost to report its merits. On *I Believe in Miracles* and *Because of Once upon a Time,* both of which have interesting melodies that make the pedestrian lyrics seem better than they are, his vocals are real attempts to showcase the tunes. Waller had no illusions about his throat—it was a lot better at swallowing than it was as a platform for song—but as a jazz musician he knew instinctively how to phrase a lyric, and his "straight" vocals on selected ballads are poignant and honorable. His tonsils were made for rasping and croaking, but in his own way he could croon.

Waller and the Rhythm's attitude toward material assigned to them can be heard in the performances they gave, both in positive and negative ways. If the group was well disposed toward a selection, the "head" arrangement was inventive and textured to the particular selection. If Waller and the group had to suffer through a ditty, their energy level dropped and the arrangement was likely to be a dead-fish satire. Two examples from the early Rhythm sessions are *Night Wind* and *Louisiana Fairy Tale.* The former is an irritatingly bathetic dirge about a lost love, and the lyrics are loaded with and-art-thou-gone pomposities. Waller plays organ on the tune, and the Rhythm—while never being obvious about it—play sanctimoniously as a means of expressing their musical contempt for the selection. Nor did the group see anything romantic or charming about *Louisiana Fairy Tale,* which describes a couple wandering about a plantation while birds tweet and dew drips from the Spanish moss. The yassuh-massa South had been under the political control of ignorant and tyrannical rednecks since the end of Reconstruction in the 1870s (in 1935 Louisiana was ruled by the brilliant and despicable Huey P. "Kingfish" Long), and northern blacks had few illusions about it. In the mid-1930s Waller remarked to Joey Nash that

> he thought it crazy [that] white folks down in Dixie paid top
> prices to see him and his crew perform, clamored for his auto-

graph, went wild over the band; while he and his group were segregated; eating in the bus, served food only on paper plates and welcomed only in colored boarding houses and hotels. Fats sagely remarked that many a colored combo went south by Greyhound and returned by bloodhound.

The Rhythm's response to *Louisiana Fairy Tale* was to play the opening statements sickly sweet, like a hotel orchestra, and to have Waller sing the words primly, until he got to the bridge:

> Is this real, this fascination?
> Are my dreams holding you fast?

Waller pronounces *fast* with a British accent—"fahst"—and then asks, "Did'ja get the 'fahst'?" He and the Rhythm knew how to assassinate a bad tune with a soft knife. The performance is successful as jazz because the band plays against the sentiments of the song, with Harry Dial's bass drum pounding away like a relentless crotch thrust, ridiculing the smarmy sentimentality of the piece, while the trumpet and reeds blow tough.

The Rhythm pulled the same trick on *Mandy,* but in a happier way, because it was a genially sentimental song, well constructed, great fun to play, and open to affectionate kidding.

Waller and the Rhythm excelled on another tune they liked—*Breakin' the Ice,* a fine example of frisky melody and witty lyrics:

> She was as cool as could be
> Though I said hello to her twice;
> Now I can take her to tea:
> Looks like I'm breakin' the ice.
>
> I call around every day
> And her people, they treat me so nice;
> They seem to think I'm okay:
> Looks like I'm breakin' the ice.
>
> Bit by bit I been makin' a hit
> [Waller revision of the lyric line:
> I'm afraid everythin's gon' be all right—
>   if you know what I mean;]

Rome, they say, wasn't built in a day
Or romance built in a night [—no].

But we saw the ring in the store;
I'm gonna save up the price;
I guess you know what it's for:
Looks like I'm breakin' the ice.

[Oh, a great big chunk—a little tiny
piece—looks like I'm breakin' the ice
—yas!]

By 1935 Waller had more than broken the ice; he had
smashed precedent: no black entertainer or musician had ever
sold as many records as he was selling, and his audience was by
no means confined to the "race" market; most of his records
were snatched up by white fans, and Victor, much to its surprise, found that it had a star on its hands. The black entertainer who appeals equally to his own and to white audiences is
a common occurrence today, but in his time Waller was a phe-
nomenon. Waller was the first black artist to "cross over" into
national popularity on a major commercial scale. He had known
for several years that Harlem loved him. Now he was to find out
that he was the darling of the nation.

12
Fractious Fingering

THE "HARMFUL LITTLE ARMFUL"—who also described himself as
the "cheerful little earful"—was familiar by face and voice to the
country by mid-1935, a year in which he had his biggest record
and appeared in two movies.

I'm Gonna Sit Right Down and Write Myself a Letter was an
unexpected "dud" from composer Fred Ahlert (*I'll Get By;
Walkin' My Baby back Home;* Bing Crosby's radio theme song,
When the Blue of the Night Meets the Gold of the Day; and
Mean to Me, which has a very Wallerish construction) and lyri-
cist Joseph Young (*Rockabye Your Baby with a Dixie Melody;
Five Foot Two, Eyes of Blue; In a Little Spanish Town; I Kiss
Your Hand, Madame; My Mammy*). Despite the credits of the
composer and the lyricist the tune aroused little interest and the
publisher hadn't made a major push on it. When a piano copy
was given to Waller at a recording session, he played it through
and found it acceptable, although he wasn't overly impressed.
He said he would get around to recording it sometime, but the
A & R man insisted that it be done immediately, so Waller and

the Rhythm worked up a simple arrangement and knocked out a performance in a casual, offhand manner, with Waller singing the vocal straight. The performance was the happiest accident of Waller's commercial career; the record sold hundreds of thousands of copies and became so closely associated with Waller that as late as 1965 a London magazine credited him as its composer. In 1936 Waller recorded another Ahlert-Young effort, *Sing an Old-Fashioned Song,* on the theory that lightning might strike twice, but Waller and the band thought this was more a case of singing a silly song, and their performance lampooned the sentiments.

Shortly after Waller shared a bill with bassist Charlie Turner's twelve-piece outfit at the Academy of Music on East Fourteenth Street in Manhattan, Phil Ponce decided to send him out on the road as a bandleader. Though Waller was never quite comfortable working with a large unit, he and the Rhythm got on well with Turner's lads and the first tour was a success. Waller also received a call from Hollywood to take a feature spot in *Hooray for Love,* in which he sang *I've Got My Fingers Crossed.* His scene, for which he collected $500, was finished in a day.

Returning to New York, Waller readied himself for another personal appearance tour that Ponce had booked. A highlight of Waller's act was a "cutting contest" on *I Got Rhythm* between Waller and pianist Hank Duncan, who had been the regular keyboard man with Turner's group. Waller would let Duncan take a chorus and then shrug to show he wasn't worried by the competition. But on Duncan's second chorus Waller would mug, his face showing surprise and concern. As trombonist Snub Mosley remembered the routine:

> Fats would let Hank play a while, and then he, would sneak up and say, "Watch out, boy, I'm gonna getcha!" . . . And you want to know something? There were a few times when he didn't catch Hank!

The routine was preserved on a 1936 recording, where the tune is taken at a furious pace and the band yells encouragement to the two pianists. As Duncan is in the middle of his chorus, Waller comments:

Aw, that's brother Duncan—he's gettin' smart, too. Hear that cat stridin' over there? Looks like he's tryin' to get somethin' from me—looks like he's tryin' to *get* somethin' from me. . . .

(Band member: Show him how to swing, Hanky.)

Aw, I ain't gonna have it. I got him some—he belongs to me. He's *mine;* he's *mine.*

(Waller begins his chorus.) There it is! Turn it loose!

As Waller nears the end of the bridge—the middle section, or "corner," of a tune which a musician has to turn in order to get back on the road of the main melody—he takes the corner on two wheels and goes up over the curb. Realizing that he has lost control, he smashes out a nonsense chord while the band huzzahs; then he gallops back to the melody to finish out his chorus. Perhaps it was exuberance that caused Waller to come undone, or the tricky arrangement, or the pace (which is too fast, making the performance a matter of calisthenics rather than music), but this was one of the few times he didn't catch Duncan or, for that matter, himself.

The recording of *I Got Rhythm* was meant to accustom the audience to Waller's appearing with a big, semiswing band in the manner of the battalions led by such stars as Benny Goodman, but the record was not issued in the United States,[22] for by that time Waller had demonstrated that his sentiments for large groups were slight, and he had also reacted to the monotony and irritations of road tours by disappearing in the middle of booking schedules, retreating to New York. Waller was slapped with several breach of contract suits and acquired a bad reputation among promoters in the East and the Midwest.

Waller's disgust and boredom with road touring will be familiar to any performer who has ever had to play a string of one-nighters, rattling from point to point in a band bus, eating cardboard food, shaking hands with local dignitaries, avoiding fights with the local troublemakers, and existing on nerves and slight

---

[22]Until the early 1970s, when it was included among the selections of a five-album series of Waller recordings from the Victor vaults, selected and programmed by Mike Lipskin.

sleep. The schedule is punishing; the demonstration of talent—
which is the performer's emotional sustenance as well as his
pride—is diluted and reduced to mechanics by constant repeti-
tion; and the tempers of the performers are quick to snap. Even
engagements of two or three weeks in one major city grow dull
and depressing. First-class talents such as Waller's live on a time
plan which always seeks the immediate, but their immediacy of
creation and/or delivery can only function in comfortable, familiar surroundings. Waller felt this immediacy only in New York
(or in fascinating new circumstances such as when he toured
Europe). The plodding, remorseless, banal atmosphere of one-
nighters drove him to drink more for escape than pleasure. Thus
his famous "acid condition," which he used as a bogus medical
excuse for sudden bolts in the middle of tours.

But despite Waller's behavior on the road, his records and
radio broadcasts were immensely popular, and late in 1935 he
was again called to Hollywood, this time for a featured role in
King of Burlesque. In this film, Warner Baxter (who starred in
the classic *42nd Street,* where he bullied winsome Ruby Keeler into
tap-dancing her way to glory) plays a Broadway producer down
on his luck. As an elevator operator in the building where Baxter maintains his offices, Waller helps organize and performs in a
show which revives Baxter's fortunes. He had dialogue as well as
music to play, and handled it well. He insisted beforehand, going over the script, that "Negroisms" be changed; his role was
originally written as an Uncle Tom type, and Waller would have
none of it. His revisions were agreed to, and he turned in a
witty, urbane performance. One movie critic wrote: "Fats Waller
lifted his eyebrow and stole the picture."

Waller's feature number in the film was *Spreadin' Rhythm
Around,* which he of all mortals knew how to do:

> Music everywhere, feet are pattin',
> Puttin' tempo in old Manhattan,
> Everybody is out high-hattin'—
> Spreadin' rhythm around.
>
> Everywhere you go, trumpets blarin',
> . . . saxophones rippin', tearin',
> Everybody you meet is rarin'—
> Spreadin' rhythm around.

Up in Harlem, in any flat,
They give you that thing
Which, accordin' to one and all,
Is what they call swing.

Those who can't afford silks and satin,
Jaded gigolos who are Latin,
Come from Yonkers, the Bronx, and Staten,
Spreadin' rhythm around.

The Jimmy McHugh-Ted Koehler tune, with its relaxed so-
phistication and teasing humor, was perfect for Waller, who—
legend says—had such a good time making his second film that
shooting was suspended for a day because he got the entire cast
loaded, as well as the director and the technicians.

Back again in New York, he became embroiled in a minor
controversy at the beginning of 1936. The estate of bandleader
and march composer John Philip Sousa was complaining
through its royalty-collection agency, ASCAP, that the late gentleman's compositions were receiving a royalty below that which
should be pegged to his august memory. ASCAP ran to Congress with the complaint, and on March 6 the affair was chron-
icled from Waller's point of view by Joseph Mitchell, a staff
reporter for the *New York World-Telegram* under the headlines:

"FLAT TIRE PAPA" ARTISTIC,
FATS WALLER TELLS CONGRESS

Negro Musician Would Like to Appear
at Inquiry—He'd Rather Testify than
Eat—And as for Sousa, Well, He Was
Good in His Way.

The article led off with a quote from E. C. Mills, general manager of ASCAP, who emoted before a House committee on pat-
ents, and expressed umbrage that

the copyright provisions specify the same remuneration to the
author of "Flat Tire Papa, Mama's Gonna Give Him Air" that
John Philip Sousa received for phonographic renditions of his
celebrated marches.

Mills' championing of Sousa was actually a case of arguing one ASCAP member's royalties against another's. Sousa had joined ASCAP in 1914; Waller in 1931. Mills apparently did not know it, or hadn't done his homework, or was feeling pressure from the Sousa estate—which in the early 1970s hired a New York publicist to spread the word that Sousa's marches, old though they might be, were not in the public domain and were still due payments for performance.

Sousa recorded for Victor in the label's early days, as did Enrico Caruso, who was offered a choice of stock in the company or cash as payment. Caruso chose cash. Seeking to promote the label, Victor tried to get crusty Sousa to endorse the company with a blanket blessing. Sousa, like Caruso, was not convinced that talking machine discs were anything more than a passing novelty, but the label persisted, and finally Sousa grudgingly mumbled, "Victor Records are all right." The statement was emblazoned in Victor advertisements in the mid-1900s as heartfelt testimony.

The *World-Telegram* article quoted Waller's response to Mills' statement and the Sousa estate's hunger:

> "Do those Congress people feel I am not as good an artist somehow as Mr. Sousa? I have always been an admirer, so to speak, of Mr. Sousa's work, too. Of course, it isn't jazz, but it's all right for that kind of stuff. To tell you the truth, I had an idea I would put that tune of his, 'The Stars and Stripes Forever,' to swing. If they mess around with me though, I won't do it. I just won't do it."

The article went on:

> Mr. Waller said he could not remember much about "Flat Tire Papa," but he is certain he wrote it for a floor-show at Connie's Inn. The lyrics were by Spencer Williams, who also wrote "I Ain't Got Nobody." Mr. Williams now lives in London, and is prospering. . . .
>
> "It was written years and years ago," said Mr. Waller. "Must have been as far back as 1928. I can't remember anything that happened away back then. Anyhow, the words would be too low-

down for you to print in your paper[23]. However, my friend, the composition was just as fine in a musical way as any of Mr. Sousa's marches the man was talking about before the Congressmen, just as fine. Mr. Sousa's marches sent men to war, but 'Flat Tire Papa' didn't. It just made people dance."

More Artistic

"Why, Fats Waller never sent no men to war. All he did was to make people dance, and stomp, and cut up. When Fats Waller sets down to a piano he don't play no simple music like marches. He just sets down and storms up a mess of jazz, which is more artistic by far."

Many jazz musicians believe that Mr. Waller is the finest swing musician in the world, but he is a modest man, and he states, "I am the finest jazz organist now alive." He is the son of the Rev. Edward Martin Waller.

"He was pastor of the First National Baptist Church, in Brooklyn, before he became deceased," said Mr. Waller. "He wanted me to play the fiddle and mess around in church, but I found my level in the cabarets. I was born in Harlem, right in the middle of it, and here I remain, happy as the day I was born, except for an acid condition that lays me up now and then."

The reporter noted that Waller's

hands are enormous. If you put gloves on [boxer] Primo Carnera's hands, they would be just about as big as Mr. Waller's, but not as competent. With them he can reach out chords on the organ or piano which most musicians would consider impossible. Recently he has been playing one-night stands, but his "acid condition" forced him to return to Harlem three weeks ago. Tonight he is leaving for Washington, where he will play in a theatre and

---

23The Harlem nightclub revues and floor shows were famous, among many reasons, for the double entendre songs, usually sung by female performers, and most often having to do with male potency, size, and acrobatics. Among the steamy ditties were such salacious items as *My Military Man; Oh, Mr. Mitchell (I'm Crazy 'bout Your Sweet Poon-Tang);* and *Do What You Did Last Night.* The songs were written by some of the best black and white talents of the day, including Harold Arlen, and sung by some of the finest performers, such as Ethel Waters.

be on hand if Congress would care to listen to him.

"I sure wish they would ask me to testify," he said, wistfully. "I'd rather testify than eat."

Through 1936 and 1937 Waller continued to record and tour, but though his records were consistently popular and audiences at live dates acclaimed him, his career was beginning to drift. His increasingly frequent hops back to Harlem in the middle of road tours gave him a bad name among promoters and bookers, and he once again fell seriously behind in his alimony payments. But he cared little or nothing about such realities. His family delighted him; he wore fine clothes; and he rode in a $7,200 custom-built Lincoln limousine. As he liked to say, "A man's best friend is his wife, his wallet, and his car."

There was also Harlem. Waller's love for the community, its music and people and life-style, was never-ending. With the rise of swing—highly arranged and danceable jazz played by big bands—the economy improved for musicians. Nearly all of the most talented black musicians lived in Harlem or passed through it on tour. One of them was the Toledo, Ohio, pianist Art Tatum, who first came to town in 1931 as an accompanist for singer Adelaide Hall, the star of the black musical *Shuffle Along* in the early 1920s. Word got around that Tatum was something special. Waller and Johnson introduced themselves backstage at the theater where Miss Hall and Tatum were appearing—would he care to come out with them and be shown the hot spots, and have a friendly drink? Tatum agreed (he was then eighteen and somewhat shy in the presence of two men he admired). They covered several saloons and clubs until they came to a small joint where a piano was handy. Waller sat down and began to play. Tatum had been maneuvered into a "cutting contest."

The lad surprised and impressed Johnson and Waller. His left hand broke the rhythm into mosaics, alternately fragmenting and reassembling it, while his right hand played complex and delicate improvisations that were sometimes so extended that it seemed he could not resolve them in time to return.

Though Tatum's first visit to Harlem was brief, by the late 1930s he was more or less headquartered there. He and Waller became pals—it was difficult for anyone, let alone a notable pianist, white or black, not to become a Waller pal—and they often toured the Harlem spots of an evening. On one occasion they appeared at a party dressed in women's clothing, with Tatum announcing himself as Mary Lou Williams and Waller taking the role of Bessie Smith, the fabulous "Empress of the Blues." While Tatum played, Waller sang, interrupting himself at one point to holler, "Mary Lou, I'm really riding, and you're not doing so bad on the keys, either."

A few years later, Waller dropped in at the famous after-hours Onyx Club on New York's "Swing Street"—Fifty-second Street between Sixth and Seventh avenues—and was happily playing for pleasure when Tatum walked in. Spying him, Waller told the customers: "Ladies and gentlemen, I play piano, but God is in the house tonight!" and turned over the keyboard to Tatum.

This is not to say that Waller admired Tatum (who always acknowledged Waller as one of his principal inspirations) more than any other pianist. If Waller had a favorite musician, it was James P. Johnson, for musical and sentimental reasons. Nor did he enjoy all keyboardists indiscriminately. He tended to admire certain features of a pianist, whether it was his (or in the case of Mary Lou Williams, her) thinking, execution, overall attitude, or grace—Earl Hines' sweep and attack, for example, or the powerful left hand of the white Arthur Schutt. Waller understood Tatum to be as much of a trailblazer for the younger generation as Johnson had been of his; but he also liked and admired Thelonious Monk and Billy Kyle, both of whom were playing an early experimental version of the avant-garde jazz that would come to be known as "bop,"[24] though Monk's compositional and concep-

---

[24]According to Oran "Hot Lips" Page, a fine trumpeter, "The word bop was coined by none other than our old friend, Fats Waller. [He] was playing with a small group at Minton's [a club which was the spawning ground for the strange new music]. Late one night some of the younger generation of musicians would bring along their instruments in the hope of jamming with the band. Waller would signal for one of them to take a chorus. The musician would start in to play, then rest for eight or twelve bars in order to get in condition for one of his crazy bop runs. Fats would shout at them, "Stop that crazy boppin' and a-stoppin' and play that jive like the rest of us guys."

tual strengths were beyond Kyle's. Both Monk and Kyle, like Tatum, were influenced by and admired Waller because they sensed his great gifts of structure—for what Waller played in after-hours joints was quite different from the happy-go-lucky bounce of his recordings. What he tossed off on recordings of mealymouthed pop songs at short notice showed only his effervescence and technique, but in the comfortable surroundings of Harlem, or in clubs like the Onyx, he played for himself, improvising tone poems and concertos rich with emotional melodies, strong and fragile all at once. This music was very different from that which the public knew as "Fats Waller."

These compositions—never recorded, never written down, but remembered with fond awe by knowledgeable musicians who heard them performed—represented Waller's delayed maturity as a musician and as a man. For most of his life he had been an overgrown and precocious kid, able to disguise his youth with gaiety, flamboyance, humor, and sheer talent. He was, for most of his career, a child prodigy of teardrop-pure innocence, wrapped in a bulk of blustering and hilarious camaraderie and sensuality, but a child still.

His attention span was that of a small boy: he wrote tunes as toys, forgetting them as quickly as they ceased to please him or to bring him quick money. He was constantly in search of adventures, but the adventures had to take place in comfortable and convivial surroundings—the company of his musical peers in Harlem, a backstage bash with cast and chorus girls, or a gargantuan eating session. Waller's high living was a succession of self-induced birthday parties. He never completed the emotional transition from childhood to maturity. At the price of preserving his childhood in alcohol, he managed to let his creative powers flow to the fullest; he was a poet, but as was true for another great American poet, Walt Whitman, the death of his mother was (in Whitman's words) "the great cloud of my life." As he grew older, the pressures of stardom and a sense of world-weariness began to affect him, though only a few close friends and associates saw it, and his private melodies, played at home or in after-hours joints, became more introspective and emotional.

But the stormy weather immediately affecting Waller had to do with his career. By 1938 he was again in debt, band bookers were leery of him because of his jumpings of dates, and his agent, Phil Ponce, was in failing health.

Once again Waller's angel's luck held. In 1935 Wallace T. "Ed" Kirkeby became Artists and Repertoire Director for Victor and began to supervise the Waller record dates. He and Waller developed a solid professional and personal relationship:

> From the control window I watched as that human volcano of energy urged on his band, and the studio rocked with the impetus of the greatest left hand in all pianodom. The great round brown face smiled across at me, and I knew that, without the slightest doubt in the world, here was a man I would love to the end of my days.

Kirkeby left Victor in 1938 to go over to the Band Booking department of the National Broadcasting Company; soon after, he was invited to join Ponce's staff. Ponce's health was ruined, and he could not cope with Waller anymore. Kirkeby took on the assignment, and as he reviewed the status of Waller's career he found an alarming picture: his new client was wanted by the Internal Revenue Service, by his first wife for back alimony, and by the Musicians' Union and several promoters, all of whom were waving legal papers and making ugly noises about money.

Kirkeby sent the Waller band on two southern tours, both of which were disasters, and although he booked Waller on some radio programs, there was not enough available work to meet Waller's price. The country seemed to have dried up, so Kirkeby took a bold but logical step: he got Waller out of the country.

13
London Suite

THE *S.S. Transylvania* slowly steamed across the Atlantic and, toward the end of her journey, lazily made her way up the River Clyde, destination Glasgow. The three most important passengers aboard, no matter what the guest list might indicate as to title, wealth, or social prominence, were Mr. and Mrs. Thomas Waller and their companion, Wallace T. "Ed" Kirkeby. By the end of the voyage, Waller was the best-known and most-liked passenger on the ship, and the salon orchestra which played for dancing held him in awe.

Casually assuring Anita Waller that there was nothing to transcontinental voyaging—he had won sea legs in 1932 with his trip to France—Waller made directly for the bar and the ship's orchestra, where he promptly converted those cautious musicians into an enthusiastic, albeit amateur, jazz band. It took only a few words from Kirkeby to convince the orchestra leader that he should let his client cozy up to the piano, and once Tom was seated at the board and his massive hands came down on the keys, the evening—and the voyage—was his.

As Tom's left hand made the rhythm throb, as his right

played frisky variations on the melody, and as his personality and drive compelled the normally stodgy ship's orchestra to work harder but feel better than they ever had before, the musical evenings aboard the *Transylvania* became the talk of the tub, and the band found itself looking forward to mounting the bandstand and welcoming the huge brown man who led them into adventures.

It was not only Waller's talent that wowed the orchestra—as well as the listeners and dancers—it was also his professional knowledge and worldly wisdom about the realities of the band business, of playing stock arrangements of polite tunes, of doing things by rote. But the man who made the piano roar convinced the group that they could do something more than meow. Even more, it was obvious that Waller was passionately in love with music, and this gave him the ability to show cautious musicians how to feel music as a romance instead of a bureaucratic sinecure.

"Don't be vague—gimme some of that fine John Haig!" he would holler at the stewards, and his glass would be refilled with the Scotch that he pronounced to be his new favorite. When the ship docked at Glasgow, a swing band led by Billy Mason welcomed the party with *Honeysuckle Rose* and the Scots gentlemen of the press impressed Waller with their ability to knock back admirable quantities of John Haig. Mason later conducted the Wallers and Kirkeby on a tour of Loch Lomond, where Waller was surprised and delighted to be hailed by a passing bicyclist who recognized him and asked for his autograph.

Waller's first appearance at the Empire Theatre brought him ten curtain calls. Next scheduled for Edinburgh, he and Kirkeby were traveling uphill in a wheeze-puff taxi when the door suddenly flew open and Waller fell out. The horrified Kirkeby stopped the cab and leaped out, only to find Waller calmly sitting on the curb: "Latch on, Mr. Kirkeby. No need to worry. I broke that fall like I learned when I was a kid—and you know I got plenty to fall on."

Kirkeby's experience and success as a manager and entrepreneur in the music business was also something for Waller to fall back on. Kirkeby had been active in the business since the teens of the century, forming a publishing business with the famous but now-forgotten vaudevillian Henry Burr, whose rendition of the tear-jerking *Old Pal, Why Don't You Answer Me?* was a specialty (in the 1920s it was sometimes sung at gangster funerals, often with the killers of the deceased joining in for the chorus). In 1917 Kirkeby was named assistant manager of the Columbia Records "recording laboratory," as studios were referred to in those days, and it is possible that he was present when the Original Dixieland Jazz Band recorded *At the Darktown Strutters' Ball.* The record was not released because the label could not overcome what it considered to be insurmountable acoustic problems—principally band member Tony Spargo's drums—and the band went to Victor, where two months later it made *Livery Stable Blues,* which caused a national sensation. In the 1920s Kirkeby parlayed the California Ramblers, a dance band, into a major group of the time. Red Nichols, Tommy and Jimmy Dorsey, and Adrian Rollini were among the many notable jazzmen Kirkeby used for recording dates; before negotiating an exclusive contract for the group with Columbia, Kirkeby recorded it under different names for seventeen labels, but fired Red Nichols because the trumpeter was doing outside free-lancing! Kirkeby also opened his own nightclub, which closed down under pressure from the Prohibition authorities, and in the 1930s he led a band billed as Ted Wallace and His Campus Boys before landing at Victor.[25] His affection for Waller was genuine, and possibly only a man of Kirkeby's temperament and experience, combined with extreme patience, could have guided Waller so well, especially since his unpredictable client sometimes sprang unwelcome surprises.

One such came during Waller's London tour of dance halls, where he had been most successful. At dawn he phoned Leslie MacDonnell, who was booking Waller's European tour (Waller was also to play Scandinavia), and told MacDonnell that he felt lonely and wanted some home cooking, that the *Queen Mary*

---

[25]At this writing (December 1976) Kirkeby is still active as a manager, spending most of his time in England with his clients, The Deep River Boys, and is a physical culture enthusiast.

was sailing that morning, and that he was going to catch the boat back to New York.

MacDonnell thought fast; instead of trying to talk Tom out of it—from the furry sound of Waller's voice, the pianist was already more than out of it, courtesy of Mr. John Haig—the promoter said he completely understood Tom's feelings, but wouldn't Tom wait long enough for MacDonnell to join him at the Palm Beach Club (where Waller was calling from) so that they might have a bon voyage drink together? For Waller to refuse would be—ahem—rude. Waller agreed and hung up. MacDonnell then made two quick calls. The first was to Ike Hatch, master of ceremonies in the Palm Beach Club; MacDonnell told him to keep Waller at the place at all costs. He then called Kirkeby, who dressed quickly and, meeting MacDonnell, rushed to the Palm Beach. As they entered, they spied Ike Hatch, who made a reassuring gesture. But Waller was not to be seen. The two men followed the slow sweep of Hatch's arm, his finger pointing to the piano. Tom was not at the instrument. He was under it, dead asleep. A seriously depleted bottle of Haig was nearby. Kirkeby and MacDonnell congratulated Hatch on a job well done.

The next evening Waller performed as scheduled at the London Palladium, but he was still woozy from the night before, so that he had to lower himself gently onto the piano stool. But he turned his condition into a joke when, after sitting down, he said to himself and the audience, "Is you all on, Fats? Yes, I sees you is," and poked his immense bottom with a forefinger, as though to help it onto the small stool.

Kirkeby, who meant to explore all possibilities to promote Waller and bring in needed cash, was interested in the possibility of a recording session in England, and had opened talks with His Master's Voice, the British division of Victor. Leonard Feather, then a young and ambitious jazz critic and enthusiast, as well as an amateur lyricist and pianist, insisted that he could collect a group of English jazzmen who could keep pace with Waller.

Six sides were made, the best of which were *Flat Foot Floogie,* a rhythm number in which Waller encouraged each musician by name as he took his solo; *A-Tisket, A-Tasket,* written by the superb singer Ella Fitzgerald, and including a Waller wisecrack, "Go find that basket, or a half pint of gin, or somethin'"; *Pent Up in a Penthouse,* written by Tom's friend and early collaborator Spencer Williams (who was living in England and in whose house Waller composed *Cottage in the Rain,* with Kirkeby supplying the title, after a gargantuan meal of real southern fried chicken); and *Music, Maestro, Please,* with Waller doubling on piano and celeste.

Ain't Misbehavin' and *Don't Try Your Jive on Me,* with Waller playing organ, were less successful: the instrument was poorly recorded, the engineer not achieving a proper sound balance. Tom's performance of *Ain't Misbehavin'* was uninspired. It was his most famous composition, with the exception of *Honeysuckle Rose,* but he had been required to sing it constantly for nearly ten years, so he approached it as a professional chore. *Don't Try Your Jive on Me,* with words by Feather, was a weak tune with pedestrian lyrics, and was probably included as a favor and thank-you to the youngster—he subsequently grew up to be a jazz critic, with all that that implies. As the English correspondent for *Metronome,* an American music magazine devoted partly to jazz, partly to large dance orchestras, and mostly to itself, Feather filed a story about the session which mentioned only *Ain't Misbehavin'* and *Jive.* A few weeks later he filed another story in which he wrote that the British jazz scene was deplorable. He subsequently made his way to America, like the French critic Hughes Panassié, where they both achieved a certain amount of notoriety and confidently wrote several silly and pontifical books about jazz and jazzmen, which were accepted by bemused Americans.

A more important session took place in August 1938. Waller's British recording dates were booked for Sundays, since that was the only day when he was not performing or partying. On August 28 he recorded six masterful and emotional pipe organ interpretations of old spirituals, in which memories of his mother and his childhood were fused with his classic taste and complete command of his favorite instrument. His essay of *Go Down, Moses* at times approaches the symphonic, and there are moments in the performance where the emotional content alternates, almost violently, between hope and rage. It had been suggested that he play *Sometimes I Feel like a Motherless Child,* and he was midway through it when he suddenly burst into tears and quit—overwhelmed by the recurring agony of the loss of Adeline Lockett Waller, and perhaps, if he saw it, the horror of her gigantic corpse being lowered in a sling from the apartment window because she was too big to fit through the door.

But he rallied soon, and called on a guest in the studio, Adelaide Hall, who had been the star of *Shuffle Along* in 1921, to sing. Memories of Broadway and Connie's Inn floor show days were easier to handle, and they recorded *That Old Feeling* and *I Can't Give You Anything but Love.*

Waller wound up the British Isles portion of his tour. He, Anita, and Kirkeby now prepared to hit Scandinavia. There was a problem in their travel arrangements, however; its name was Hitler. In order to be in Copenhagen for the first scheduled appearance, the Waller party would have to begin their train travel in Holland on a German passenger express, Mitropa, then change to a Danish line at Hamburg. At first, Waller refused, saying, "That rascal don't like me, my color, or my music." But Kirkeby, who spoke enough German to pass them through customs points, made arrangements for Tom and Anita to remain in their locked compartment until the moment of the change-over.

The plan worked well enough until the Mitropa arrived in Hamburg, early in the morning. As Kirkeby was escorting the Wallers to breakfast at a restaurant on the station platform, a squad of Wehrmacht soldiers tramped by, bound for a troop train. Waller panicked, but Kirkeby took his arm and they quickly boarded the Danish train.

The Scandinavian tour was successful but by late September Hitler had bluffed the pigeon-livered British and French governments into believing that he was prepared to go to war over the Sudetenland, the German-speaking population of Czechoslovakia. The Waller party returned to England, where Tom played a few dance hall dates and made an experimental television appearance with the British Broadcasting Corporation.

The trio boarded the *Île de France,* which plowed rough seas that knocked out most of the passengers but bothered Tom not at all; the absence of other customers at the saloon gave him room to take on a sea chest worth of excellent liquor and food.

Back in New York, Waller and Kirkeby collected the personnel of the Rhythm again, and settled in for a three-month run at the Yacht Club on "Swing Street."

The European tour had been an enormous personal and prestigious success, and had brought in enough money for Waller to buy a house in the St. Albans section of Queens. James P. Johnson had been in semiretirement in his house since the Depression, concentrating on composing symphonies, ballet scores, tone poems, and folk operas. As James P.'s wife, Mae Wright, recalled:

> I sold Fats his house—just a few blocks from ours, and every once in a while he'd come in at four or five in the morning to go to bed here. He'd say, "The kids too noisy over at my house."

This was Waller's way of saying that he wanted to work out some of his private ideas for composition but didn't want to disturb his children's sleep. From the early 1920s, when Tom had been James P.'s student, the Johnsons had been used to having Waller fuss and fox around on James P.'s piano in the predawn hours.

There were other occasions when his children were present at his early morning workshops. His son Maurice recalled:

> When I was seven or eight I used to sit listening to him play the piano at home until four in the morning sometimes. That's when he wasn't entertaining, just playing. From those evenings I know what he was trying to say. His ability and technique were overpowering. . . .
>
> My father spent a lot of time composing things that have never been published. . . . They weren't commercial. . . . It was a matter of getting at his inner self in them.

Waller's engagement at the Yacht Club was the longest he ever spent in any one spot, with the exception of the year in

Cincinnati, so he found more time to play his experimental melodies and tone poems. He was also available to the press, which was becoming more interested in him, and in a November 11 interview for the *World-Telegram* he elaborated on some of the aspects of European life that most impressed him. The article's quotations were prefaced by the statement: "It is a fact that many patrons [at the Yacht Club] stop dancing when Fats and his band go into their stuff, preferring to listen—an unusual tribute."

"Throughout the British Isles and Scandinavia audiences like to listen," said Fats. "Unlike the jitterbugs over here, they will often stop while dancing as a band builds up to the climaxes. I never saw such an intelligent appreciation of swing. After one concert I gave in Sweden a chap came up to me and said: 'What did you play in that seventeenth bar of the fourth chorus?' He killed me, but it's typical of the response you get."

Know Their Stuff

Fats says it is because they study American records. "Really study them," says Fats. "They will play a phrase over and over again, and then they'll say, 'Well, no, that isn't right'—and they'll go ahead and write in their own arrangement, and all I heard were better.

"Why, in any of the English spots where they have good orchestras . . . sometimes they'll play Bach, Mozart, Brahms, and first thing you know they'll slide gently into swing, and it kills you. And they take our popular stuff and make it interesting, make it amusing, too." . . .

"For years I have been trying to sell the idea of softer stuff over here, but I have never been able to get away with it until now," says Fats. "I used to tell 'em down at Victor I ought to tone down, but they'd just say, 'No, go ahead and give 'em that hot primitive stuff; that is what they want.' But I don't think so any more," says Fats. "I think Europe's way is the right way, and I think it'll take over here, and I hope it does before we lose our eardrums."

In Glasgow, Fats got a shock he is still recovering from. "Somebody brought up to me an old record I'd made, oh, years and years ago, an old 'St. Louis Blues' record on the organ. And this guy says, 'In the middle of this record are two bars of a Bach chorale; how do you explain that?' Well, I just couldn't explain it. In fact, I'm still trying to figure it out—how two bars of a Bach chorale got into the 'St. Louis Blues.' It must have been one of those nights," said Fats.

The interview was a classic example of the dilemma of the superior American jazzman who rightly feels a kinship with and appreciation for other musical forms; who is artistically ambitious and explorative; who feels his creative impulses tethered by commercial music which, though it pays his rent and—in Waller's case—makes him a star, impinges upon his private time; and who is surprised and delighted by the sometimes ludicrous seriousness and respect with which the foreign jazz fan and critic approach the music and American artists.

Though Waller was generous to European attitudes and opinions in late 1938, he had a more practical sight on them at the beginning of that year, before his overseas tour. In an interview published on January 15—again in the *World-Telegram,* which seems to have taken a particular and continuing fancy for Tom since the 1920s—he said:

"I am nobody to get mighty about swing. . . . I think it is just a musical phase of our social life. Nobody can tell what swing really is." . . .

Most everybody knows that Fats is regarded by many as the nation's No. 1 swing pianist, but most everybody does not know that in this field of prima donnas he is so regarded even by his confreres. Fats, who is a modest and genial chap and who will beat up a piano in his own home for the fun of it, curls up when you ask him how he got that way.

"Why, Eddie Schutt [Arthur "The Baron" Schutt, a white pianist with a good reach in his left hand and a sideman on the 1920s sessions by Red Nichols and His Five Pennies] plays a terrific piano out on the Coast. . . . Classic, swing—call your shot— Eddie can play it. When you hear a piano—and what I mean a piano!—in the films and don't see the player that's Eddie. Bert Shefter—have you heard his 'Scandal in A Flat'? Terrific."

The "Scandal in A Flat" swings one of the Chopin impromptus, which suggests to Fats that swing is developing into a satire—sometimes clever, as when Reginald Forsythe, the astonishing London Negro, arranges the music on classical compositions.

"I am nobody to get mighty about swing. . . . But to take the classic composers and toss 'em around, after all, does call attention to Bach and Schubert and Chopin of people who think they're movie stars, wrestlers or Fordham [University football team] guards."

Tom revealed an amused and bemused tolerance for European fanatics, as compared to American dance fans he had seen, having just returned from a West Coast engagement:

"The Coast is mad about swing . . . madder even than in Paris and over there, boy, they're just clean crazy. . . .

"All the Paris swing nuts know one another and assemble at one another's homes for what they call 'tea concerts.' You'll get a call in the afternoon:—'I just got half a dozen records from America. Come on over.' And over they come, just like as if they were going to Carnegie Hall. Plain nuts."[26]

The Yacht Club engagement ended in mid-January 1939, when Kirkeby pulled the band out after a dispute with the club owners. Tom and the Rhythm worked fill-in dates for the next few months, until Kirkeby received word that England would

---

[26]It was, for many years, a sanctimonious pleasure for European critics to explain jazz in terms of lopsided, unfair, and troubled American race relations. This afforded overseas critics, as well as fanatical American cultists, an opportunity to apply a "scientific," blanket-formula explanation to a spiritual affair, to encase an abstract in concrete rules. The false theory was at one time highly popular, but in the case of the European critics, the lofty condemnation was based in part on the absence of comparable race problems in their own nations. By the late 1960s, when France was feeling the effects of North African Islamic minorities and Britain was attempting to deal with its tremendous influx of West Indian émigrés, both countries discovered—much to their chagrin—that they too had race problems. So the elder generation of jazz critics, who were young and feisty in the 1930s and 1940s, sang soft in the 1970s, for by that time it was apparent that the United States had reached, if not a solution, at least a workable truce in its race relations.

welcome another Waller tour. He and Tom set sail in the spring.

On the way over, Kirkeby and Waller discussed, as a fancy, an improvised suite based on impressions of certain sections of London, with Kirkeby providing basic descriptions and Waller taking off on the loose themes supplied. The subject was forgotten until a morning when, having arrived in England, Waller was due to make some private recordings. But on that particular morning the composer had a boiling stomach brought on by a more than usually luxurious "liquid ham and eggs" breakfast—two four-finger shots of whiskey. Tom arrived at the studio with a clutch of the intestines and a desire to sleep or be gloriously sick.

But Kirkeby perked him up with the suggestion that this would be an opportune moment to fly away on the impressions of London life they had discussed. As always, when musical adventure or challenge called, Tom rallied. Kirkeby again gave brief, succinct descriptions of the regions to be portrayed: Piccadilly, Chelsea, Soho, Bond Street, Limehouse and Whitechapel.

Acting on Kirkeby's synopses, Tom recorded what was to be known as the *London Suite* on April 3, 1939. Kirkeby was so enthusiastic that he wanted Waller to go to His Master's Voice and re-record the *Suite* in a professional recording studio, which Tom did, on June 13. Plans were made to release the June 13 masters commercially, but Great Britain's entry into World War II in September 1939 canceled the project. The masters were "lost" until 1948, when Kirkeby, returning to Britain as manager of another act, happened by accident to find test pressings of the June sessions in a music publisher's office. They were subsequently released in the 1950s.

What is important about the *London Suite* is not Waller's impression of English life—the *Piccadilly* portion is not about Piccadilly but about Harlem, and *Bond Street*, portraying the customer's row of whores, could as easily be placed in Hazel Valentine's Daisy Chain bordello—but that Waller is free to play a sampling of the private, even furtive, ideas that came to dominate his musical thinking as he grew older.

The introspective, shy, and hurt sentiments of *Chelsea* and *Whitechapel* represent the only recorded examples of Waller's private emotions and demonstrate his fondness for romantic classical piano expression. There are moments of Mozart, Chopin, and Brahms—as well as Paderewski, James P. Johnson, and perhaps most of all, Adeline Lockett Waller—in the *London Suite*. It is a moving performance, containing some of Waller's finest melodies, and it offers a rare glimpse of the furtive tenderness that animated Waller at heart—in his words, the "fine Arabian stuff that your dreams is made of."

14
Slightly Less Than Wonderful

ON A SPRING EVENING IN 1941 in Kansas City, Missouri, if one happened to be passing by the local theater that served as a dance hall, one might have seen a bus parked by the side entrance displaying signs in the rear windows that read: "Fats Waller and His Orchestra." One might also have observed a dapper, slim white man approaching middle age—Kirkeby—trying to calm down a large, enraged brown man—Waller—while the fifteen members of the band leaned or slumped disconsolately against the walls of the theater or stretched their legs or made resigned faces. Approaching closer, one might have heard the furious Waller's conclusion of his jeremiad: "This business would turn the stomach of a goat!"

One would then have seen Waller stomp angrily off, yelling over his shoulder that he was going to look up his good friend Bill "Count" Basie, whose band was headquartered in Kansas City, and go get crocked for spite.

The incident which made the normally tolerant and whimsical Waller explode was the last of a chain of aggravating insults, disappointments, and stupidities which characterized all of his one-night-stand road tours. The band had just completed a trip of 643 miles from Denver, only to find that the date in Kansas City had been canceled because the promoter had not paid a deposit on the theater.

There were other incidents on his road tours that often led, sometimes quite justifiably, to Waller's bolting back to New York. On a date in Mississippi, where the band was booked at a backwoods affair, local white apes slashed the tires of Waller's car and poured sand in the gas tank. Hotel accommodations for the band were simply not possible down South, so the musicians had to be put up in private homes. They were denied meals in restaurants, and gas stations sometimes refused to service "Old Methusela," as the bus was nicknamed. During a local tour in Florida, Kirkeby attempted to charter a private railroad car for the band so that the players would not be disturbed, but when they arrived in Jacksonville the railroad management took one look at the sixteen black customers and said that no cars were available. On still another occasion the band arrived at a club in time to see it still being built! Local sheriffs were especially obnoxious and hostile, and usually very quick to demonstrate that they were heavily armed.

Although Waller's road tours were usually relieved by two-, three-, or even six-week engagements at big-city hotels and clubs, most of his work on the road consisted of grueling and infuriating one-nighters, usually promoted by quick-buck local sharpies who sometimes refused to pay the band after the performance and then called in the law to run it out of town. Though Kirkeby tried to avoid hop-along tours, especially through the South, he was faced with the continuing problem of bringing in enough money to keep Waller temporarily solvent and to make some headway on Waller's bills to the Internal Revenue Service, his ex-wife, and other debtors. Kirkeby's problem was complicated by Tom's penchant for spending wildly; among Waller's many talents was one for living beyond his means. Kirkeby always had an eye out for a major break that would advance Waller's prestige and price, but to make do he had to run races so that he and Waller could stay even with themselves.

In order to increase Waller's drawing power, Kirkeby persuaded him to front a large group on the road, playing "swing" arrangements in the manner of other large jazz/dance orchestras, such as Benny Goodman, Artie Shaw, and Tommy Dorsey. Waller complied, but the six-man group still prevailed for most of his Rhythm recording dates, and the small band setup remained Tom's favorite.

One of Waller's more pleasant interludes while on the road in 1941 was a two-week stand at the Paramount Theatre in Los Angeles, where he shared top billing with Eddie "Rochester" Anderson, a rasp-voiced and gifted actor, comic, and dancer, who was a featured and highly prized regular member of the cast of the Jack Benny weekly radio program on the National Broadcasting System, of which Victor Records was a subsidiary. Taking advantage of the tie-in, Victor often arranged for Waller's long-run hotel appearances to be broadcast as "remotes" on Saturday nights, and while Waller was on the West Coast it put together an interview feature:

Announcer: At this time we have the pleasure of bringing to our microphone a gentleman who has been the idol of the nation's dance fans for a good many years—Fats Waller. Usually a solo entertainer, Fats has recently branched out into the field of orchestra leading, and hopes to acquire as much fame with his band as he has with his individuality. As most of you know, he is a man of somewhat large proportions, standing 5 feet 10½ inches high, and weighs 265 pounds. But he does have the jovial personality that is supposed to be one of the characteristics of the corpulent people. As a special feature on this program, I'd like to introduce, as master of ceremonies, a man who is partly responsible for Jell-O[27] finding its way into millions of American homes—none other than Jack Benny's right-hand man, Rochester. So if you'll take over from here Rochester, I know the next few minutes will be something we'll never forget.

Ro: Well, Fats, I got a few questions here to ask you. You all ready with the answers?

---

[27]Jell-O, a gelatin dessert mix, was the sponsor of the Jack Benny radio program.

FW: Well, go ahead and shoot 'em at me, Rochester; I'll see if I can shoot as much bull as you can.

Ro: How'd you happen to start your musical career?

FW: Well, they stopped me swingin' in church, so I had to swing outside somewhere.

Ro: Have you ever worked in any other job besides musical ones?

FW: Oh, yes, I had all kinds of jobs. I was an errand boy. . . . I used to steal quite a number of cookies when I was a grocer's errand boy. I think that accounts for my weight bein' so corpulent.

Ro: Yeah, yeah, I see.

FW: You dig?

Ro: Yeah, them cookies.

FW: Them cookies, man, Grandma's cookies.

Ro: With sugar on 'em?

FW: With *plenty* of sugar.

[Waller and Rochester laugh; there is also background laughter from band members in the studio.]

Ro: What instruments do you play?

FW: Piano, violin, and organ.

Ro: Well, gee, that violin is—

FW: No, no, no, no. Lemme tell you about that violin episode right now. I played violin in the school orchestra and played it so terribly that the boys used to—when I start playin' a solo—they'd say, "Hey, give that rat some cheese."

[Background laughter.]

Ro: Well . . . we can class your violin playin' with another violinist[28] that I happen to know. . . .

FW: Oh-oh! That sounds bad.

[Rochester and Waller laugh.]

Ro: Has the draft affected your band yet?

FW: No, the draft hasn't affected the band yet. The boys have their overcoats for the draft.

Ro: Okay, well, we'll leave the window open. . . . When you organized your first band, did you pattern your style after any particular band of that time?

FW: No, when I started that first band, it was every man for hisself and every tub on its own bottom.

Ro: Why did you choose this particular selection?

FW: What selection?

Ro: The one that you call your theme song.

FW: Ohhhh—well, I tell you, that was written—our theme song bein' *Ain't Misbehavin'*—that was written while I was lodging, or, rather, *incarcerated* in the alimony jail, and I wasn't misbehavin'—you dig?[29]

---

[28]One of Benny's running gags was his haughtiness about his off-key violin playing.

[29]Waller also claimed that *My Fate Is in Your Hands* was written in the slammer, although his lyricist on those melodies, Andy Razaf, had different and probably more accurate versions. Waller like to ring in apocryphal stories of his cell time, partly for laughs, partly as a protest over his continuing alimony situation.

[Background Laughter.]

    Ro: Yeah, yeah. . . .

    FW: Well, all right.

    Ro: How many recordings have you made; can you give me an idea?

    FW: Well, roughly between 800 and 1,000 records.

    Ro: How 'bout after you smooth it out?

    FW: When you smooth it out, we made at least twenty to thirty records—and when you *really* smooth it out, we *did* make a couple last week.

    Ro: When you go to a new engagement, how much time do you spend rehearsin'?

    FW: We *don't* rehearse. . . . in fact, we close tonight and open tomorrow.

    Ro: Yeah, I didn't think you had to rehearse.

    FW: That's it.

    Ro: That's right.

    FW: You rehearse on the job at the public's expense.

    Ro: When you have an engagement that gives you a lot of free time, what do the boys in the band do to pass away the free time?

    FW: Why, you can catch them guys playin' five-card, rummy, "21.". . . Somebody's in here hollerin' "Shhhh!" . . . I dunno who's doin' it. . . .

[Background laughter.]

Ro: What has been the greatest contributing factor to your success?

FW: My wife, I believe.

Ro: Ah, that's fine, that's fine.

FW: She stuck with me through thick and thin, you know, she was right along with me, everything was goin' so good. She was my pal and buddy, and she kept encouragin' me. Finally, I got near the jackpot—I haven't hit it *yet,* but I hope to in the near future.

Ro: What advice would you give to a young musician who is starting to organize his first band?

FW: . . . start from the bottom up and work like a son of a gun.

Ro: What is your personal opinion of the boogie-woogie type of music?

FW: "Beat me, daddy, eight to the bar."[30]

[Laughter.]

Listen, Rochester, a fella was tellin' me this afternoon that he had a new song out, so I asked him the title of it. It's one of those boogie tunes . . . somethin' about "What does the termite say to the bartender?" . . . said somethin' about, "Beat me, daddy, I just ate the bar."

[Laughter.]

Ro: Do you think that swing, as it is played today, will always have a place in the musical world?

---

[30]A catchphrase from a pop song of the time. Waller was being politely evasive in his quotation of it; he held an abiding contempt for the style, once describing it to his friend Joey Nash as "thirty-two bars of absolutely nothing."

FW: I think that swing will be here forever and a day, without a letup.

Ro: You think swing is here to sway?

FW: Sway and stay.

Ro: What has been the most outstanding incident in your musical career?

FW: The most outstanding incident . . . *let* me see. Well, I'll tell you one thing; when I was over in Manchester, England, in 1939,[31] I fell out of a cab door.

Ro: I imagine . . .

FW: We were doin' about thirty miles an hour. I didn't get a scratch.

Ro: Well, that was an incident. Do you have any hobbies?

FW: Hobbies? Ohhhh, yes. I got one hobby I can't tell the people about over this air. . . .

Ro: Do you participate in any . . . sports?

FW: Oh, well, nooo. . . . I wouldn't say I participate—ever seen two little cubes that jump around?

Ro: Wellll . . .

FW: I participate *sometimes.* Most of the time I have to stay away 'cause they'll keep me *broke* if I stick to 'em. . . .

Ro: . . . You know, Fats—gee whiz, I can think of the first time I saw you; that was my first opportunity to get to New York, some time ago. . . . you sat down at that organ and started beating out—you know, I didn't have any idea that that kind of music could come out of an organ!

---

[31]Waller was hazy on the date of this incident; it took place in Scotland the year before.

FW: Ooooh, yes. All you gotta do is put your hands on it and get that right ticklin' rhythm, and it's on. The ball really starts to roll. . . .

By January 1942, it appeared that Waller was starting to roll in the direction that Kirkeby wanted him to. A Carnegie Hall solo recital was produced, in which Tom was intended to demonstrate that he was a serious artist as well as a master entertainer. The program called for the first half of the concert to feature Waller as piano and organ soloist, playing the *London Suite* as well as variations on classical themes and motifs. The second half of the concert would present Waller in a jazz session with selected players, among them trumpeter Oran "Hot Lips" Page. As a special fillip, the surviving members of the white "Austin High Gang" of the 1920s were to appear in a jam session. The alumni included Gene Krupa, lately featured with Benny Goodman's band and at that time the best-known drummer in the country.

The result was an uncomfortable and slightly embarrassing failure. Perhaps Waller was too excited about the prospect of being considered a serious artist, or too nervous, or too casual, but his performance was wayward and—most unusual for him—sloppy.

Both Eddie Condon, the white banjoist/guitarist who worked with Waller on the 1929 *Harlem Fuss/Minor Drag* session, and Eugene Sedric recalled that the backstage area was piled high with musicians, friends, and well-wishers, and that Waller was, despite his enormous capacity for and experience with happy waters, drunk. "Everybody got half-high, and it turned out to be kind of a clambake," Sedric said, while Condon remembered that at an early point in the first half of the program Tom played Gershwin's *Summertime* on the organ and that whatever tune he played after that, it wound up being *Summertime*.

Although Waller was the first jazz musician to give a solo recital at Carnegie Hall, he was not the first jazz musician to appear there. In 1928 there had been a program of the blues music of W. C. Handy, and Waller had substituted for James P. Johnson as soloist in the performance of Johnson's *Yamerkraw* suite. In 1938, as a publicity stunt, Benny Goodman's orchestra

gave a concert which was nationally noted—and fussed over in
conservative quarters—as a landmark of "native" American
music being played in the palace of classical concerts. Recitals
by jazz musicians, not to mention pop musicians, have been a
semiregular feature of Carnegie since it ceased to the premiere
prestige hall in New York, but in 1942 such an appearance by a
jazzman—and a black to boot—was a novelty.

Moreover, in 1942 there was a growing acceptance among major newspapers and magazines—what would now be called The
Media—to accept and treat jazz as a popular entertainment
form in which standards of excellence could be found, such as
those that had been found twenty years earlier in the stage musical and the motion picture. Waller was a lovable and highly
popular figure, as well as being immensely gifted—Oscar Levant,
the flamboyant pianist and interpreter of Gershwin, had publicly
named Waller "the black Horowitz," after Vladimir Horowitz, a
classical pianist of mighty technique and wide fame who, in the
words of Professor Johannes Lemke of the Peabody Conserva-
tory of Music in Baltimore, played "faster and louder and more
accurately than anybody else, though he had none of Waller's
soul."

But the concert was an artistic failure, which is to say that it
was a personal and professional failure for Waller. It was an
isolated flop, doing neither Waller's career nor a belief in jazz
any harm, but a poor showing nonetheless.

Of the reviews that appeared, that of the *New York Times*
went out of its way to be kind and considerate, but was forced
by candor to write up the recital as an uncomfortable write-off:

FATS WALLER HEARD
IN CARNEGIE RECITAL

2,600 Attend Event Given
by Pianist, Composer and Leader

Thomas (Fats) Waller, who has contributed mightily to Ameri
can jazz as a pianist, singer, composer, personality and band
leader, last night gave a solo recital at Carnegie Hall.

The news is bad. The program, according to a note by John
Hammond, was dedicated to Fats' artistry as a musician and

composer, and the pianist apparently took this seriously. Instead of being his buoyant, rhythm-pounding self, he improvised soulfully, for long stretches at a time, first on the piano and then on the Hammond electric organ. Long pauses between his groups did not help matters.

There was a near-capacity audience of 2,600 which was more than ready to be pleased. It applauded when a recognizable melody emerged in the rambling improvisations. It even began to "get hep" when Fats started his improvisation on eight bars from Elgar's "Pomp and Circumstance" on the organ. But Fats stopped playing with a swinging rhythmic bass, and went off into fancy ornamental figures again and the audience relapsed.

Half an hour later when he started playing in jazz style again during "I'm Gonna Sit Right Down and Write Myself a Letter," the audience started beating its feet and tapping its palms to get him started.[32] But to no avail. After a twenty-three minute intermission the audience just sat numbly through a long "London Suite" and the succeeding variations on a Tchaikovsky Theme which was indistinguishable from the suite.

The *New York Daily News,* the city's most popular paper, suffered from a low rating for its reviews of "art" performances; its judgments of plays and concerts were considered more valuable commercially (if favorable) than for their insight or grace. With a sometimes well-grounded suspicion of highfalutin, fancy, tuxedo affairs, the paper took a you-can't-fool-me attitude toward such presentations. As usual, the *Daily News* combined a modicum of common sense with a belligerent denunciation of things it did not care to understand, and Douglas Watt's review, while dismissing Waller as an amusing black, slashed at jazz itself:

> Well, they did it. Hoping to prove that Thomas (Fats) Waller is a great artist, some well-wishers put the hefty, chucklesome colored jive pianist up on the stage of Carnegie Hall last night. They gave him a piano and an organ to play with and conjured up a full house.
>
> Along about the 66th chorus of "Honeysuckle Rose," things

---

[32]The *New York Times* being—then as now—a somber oracle, it was presumably forbidden for a *Times* writer to descend to the vulgar "clapping their hands."

became a little blurred. It wasn't Fats' fault, understand. They
had asked for it and with graciousness and obvious pleasure, he
was indulging his passion for cute, ornamental effects, letting his
imagination run riot and pulling all the stops of his engaging, but
limited, technique. . . .

Just one thing more. When they try to tell you that the little
smoky music with the cute shapes is our native art, our own muscular music, tell them to cut it. Don't let 'em woo you with that.

Next week: Bill Robinson[33] in "Hamlet."

While the *Times* reluctantly identified Waller as the cause of
the evening's disappointment and the *News* regarded him as a
genial dupe of sinister forces attempting to make a saint of a
minstrel show piano pounder in the cause of a suspect music, it
was oddly given to the *Daily Worker* to make an accurate, if
peripheral, observation.

The *Daily Worker* (now the *Daily World*) was, and is, the
mouthpiece of the pro-Moscow Communist Party of the United
States, slavishly following the Kremlin's strategic and tactical
directives and policies. In 1942 the normal harpings of the
Worker against capitalist America were muted because of the
alliance of Russia, the United States, and Great Britain against
Nazi Germany, but it was still permissible to score propaganda
points. Thus O. V. Clyde spent much of the large space allotted
his review of the Waller concert in decrying segregational "Jim
Crow" attitudes which prevented black and white musicians
from appearing together in public performance, although such
appearances were no longer unusual. Benny Goodman, the
"King of Swing," had, some five years earlier, announced to the
music business and the nation that black xylophonist Lionel
Hampton and black pianist Teddy Wilson were in his band to
stay as long as they cared to, and that he was honored to have
them.

Clyde's review avoided any assignment for the failure of the
concert to Waller personally—where, in fact, it belonged—and
he humphed and phumphed over jazz itself, implying that it was

---

[33]Bill "Bojangles" Robinson was a sensational dancer and entertainer and
one of the great black stars of the day.

an entirely black creation to which practicing white musicians might, on good behavior, be admitted. But he made an astute comment, momentarily shedding Marxist ideology, about the people who had come to see the recital, and his observations are still applicable, particularly in the rock 'n' roll era:

> The audience was a study. It deserves credit for honoring Fats Waller and his associates. But it was an uncritical audience, an audience autointoxicated by an unmistakable cultism which blurred its discriminations so that it laughed at the wrong things and at the wrong time.
>
> It is quite possible for the exquisite art of jazz to develop its own snobberies and orthodoxies which are concealed under the banner of a revolt against the "classical" concert hall and its accompanying philistinisms. A noticeable philistinism is present when ordinary trills, *sforzandi* effects and *glissandi* on organ keys are ovationed as big discoveries. One of the rending things about the fight which musicians like Mr. Waller and his colleagues have to make to win the appreciation they deserve is that they have to train even their own friends to understand what they are doing.

Waller, so far as is known, shrugged off the Carnegie fiasco, and remembered it only as a "Killer Diller from Manila" evening where he was surrounded by plenty of friends, with plenty to drink and laugh about. Despite the poor reviews and the tepid audience reaction Waller received quite a lot of publicity from the nonevent, and Kirkeby, being a professional, subscribed to the truism that bad or lukewarm publicity was still, after all, publicity.

Waller went back on the road immediately after the Carnegie date. In Chicago he opened the new Down Beat Room, playing there four weeks and touting a new young blues singer named Dinah Washington, whom he had discovered. She later went on to a solid career as a jazz and pop vocalist. In Minneapolis, Kirkeby arranged for Waller to meet with Dimitri Mitropoulos, a classical pianist and conductor whom Waller much admired. The two spent a relaxed afternoon together, taking turns at the piano and discussing music. Mitropoulos was scheduled to conduct a Swing Parade Concert at a serviceman's benefit, and

Waller eagerly joined the company, consisting of over a hundred musicians and the United States Navy Chorus, as they thundered out *Anchors Aweigh* and the *Star-Spangled Banner*.

The benefit was one of literally hundreds that Waller played— for free—to support the American war effort. Patriotism, in those days and at that time, was not something to be dismissed by professors, newspaper columnists, and social reformers as misplaced and misused childish emotion. Tom had a large heart, and a generous portion of it went to his country. He went to great lengths—even dangerous ones, where his health was concerned—to play for black and white servicemen. He remembered his brother Robert fighting in World War I, and his own son Thomas (by his first wife, Edith), was a corporal in the Army. He also remembered being surprised at the Hamburg railway station platform by a squad of goose-stepping Hun soldiers in 1938, and he looked forward to "that rascal Hitler" being whipped.

In addition to his harum-scarum professional schedule— "Wherever the work was," Kirkeby said, "that's where we went"—Tom was so quick to accept requests to appear at servicemen's clubs and spent so much energy on these performances that Kirkeby began to wonder whether even his client's amazing stamina could carry him through. The year before, after taking a complete physical examination, Waller was bluntly told by his physician that if he didn't lay off the drinking he would kill himself. In a rare stretch of common sense, Tom followed orders and went on the wagon, limiting himself to soda pop and not allowing even the pressures of the road, his crazy travel schedule, or the convivialities of recording sessions to tempt him. For a brief period it was Waller, Waller everywhere, nor any drop to drink. But the soda pop—which he ordered by the case—gave way to cases of wine, which he considered a light refreshment, and soon after that his experiment in abstinence was abandoned.

Another comfort also most dear to Waller was reluctantly abandoned in the autumn of 1942. The last recording session by the small-group Rhythm was held on July 13. Later that year the American Federation of Musicians went on strike and refused to record without a wage increase; as union members,

Waller and the Rhythm were compelled to comply. Then the government placed a wartime emergency restriction on new recordings. The metal used for matrix stampers, from which commercial copies were pressed, could better be used for war industry raw material. Finally, Kirkeby's ultimate concern was to "continue the battle to get Fats out of the red." Waller could play anywhere as a single, using local musicians for backup if they were required, and the tightened wartime economy made the Rhythm an expense which approached luxury. The group was disbanded with regret on all sides.

The wartime recording ban did, however, produce a notable incident. The government was constantly urging citizens to save any and all objects that could conceivably be used in the manufacture of needed weaponry or military support hardware. "Scrap metal" drives were a common feature of the war years, and the items collected included used tin cans. The government feared that careless citizens might include in their garbage tin cans which could be pounded into reborn metal that might eventually become tanks, airplanes, bayonets, canteens, or triggers. Hoping to educate the homeowner on how to cull his slops for precious metals, the government asked Waller to write a cheerful, swinging ditty as part of its promotional campaign, advising the citizen that turning in such refuse would count as a credit on his food-rationing coupons. Tom gladly obliged, and in short order dashed off and recorded a catchy tune entitled *Get Some Cash for Your Trash*. The government declared itself pleased, and the tune was given wide publicity. All was bliss until Washington discovered that "trash" was Harlem slang for what whores peddle. Thereupon, the government summarily abandoned its attempt to manipulate the hit parade.

15
The Jackpot

THE PORTRAYAL of the black on film has seldom been accurate, whether the movies were made by white or by black directors. Until the 1950s the black, with rare exceptions, was presented as a jolly nitwit and used for comic relief. In the 1920s independent black filmmakers operating on shoestring budgets turned out potboilers for consumption in Negro theaters, and in the 1930s some white studios remade successful features with all-black casts, booking the films only to theaters in black city neighborhoods. Rarely did a major artist like Paul Robeson appear in a powerful, serious film like *The Emperor Jones,* shot from the stage play by Eugene O'Neill (and a portrait resembling some present-day extremist black politicos and dictators).

Yet there were occasional films in which black performers were given an opportunity to demonstrate their considerable skills. Canada Lee, a fine actor who starred in Broadway productions of *Macbeth* and *Native Son,* the latter based on Richard Wright's[34] angry novel, and both directed by Orson Welles,

---

[34]Wright, like W. E. B. DuBois and Paul Robeson, so despaired of the social situation of blacks that he turned to Communism. All three were used by the CPUSA as valuable propaganda tools. Robeson, who died in the 1970s, believed until the end that Stalin was a swell fellow.

was featured in a 1938 film, *They Won't Forget,* an adaptation of a true incident, the 1913 lynching of a Jewish factory superintendent, Leo Fuchs, in Georgia, accused of raping a white fourteen-year-old employee. In 1936, Hattie McDaniel, playing a southern mammy in *Gone with the Wind,* won the Academy Award for the best supporting actress. There were even rewards for the connoisseur in low-budget pictures: the Charlie Chan detective series of the 1940s, programmers playing as second features, introduced the character of Birmingham Brown, Chan's chauffeur and comic sidekick to Chan's "number one son." Brown was played by the great Mantan Moreland, and without the series there would be little if any film record of black vaudeville performing techniques, long since a lost art.

The characterization of the black American in recent films, in which he is depicted as hip, slick, brutal, usually earning his living outside the law, and delighting in the killing of white people, who are always cast as crooked cops or Mafia goons, is as wayward as the "handkerchief head" stereotypes of the 1920s, 1930s, and 1940s. The casting of black actors meant to represent black Americans as recognizable *Americans* was largely limited to the decade of the 1950s, with the gifted James Edwards appearing in many memorable performances—*Home of the Brave, Steel Helmet, The Killing*—and the rising stars of young Sidney Poitier and Harry Belafonte.

But in the 1940s, Hollywood, for commercial reasons, began to consider the possibility of attracting white audiences with all-star black features. The experiment was unsuccessful, but *Stormy Weather* did leave a lavish film testament to the superb talents of Bill "Bojangles" Robinson, as well as give Tom Waller a notable spot.

The plot was virtually nonexistent: it consisted of the mild trials of a troupe of black performers putting on a hit Broadway musical. What few dramatics there were consisted of the love interest between Robinson and Lena Horne, whose very name is a superlative. Miss Horne's voice and face have always been regally beautiful and have defied time. In 1943, when *Stormy Weather* was made, she was in her twenties. Robinson was quite obviously in his fifties, and their scripted love match was ludicrous, but the purpose of the film was to show a lot of singing and dancing; character relationships were haphazard and off-hand.

Waller appears in the first half of the film. He is "discovered" leading a small band in a bistro when the Broadway-bound troupe enters for an evening's entertainment. Waller and the band play behind singer Ada Brown in a feeble blues, *That Ain't Right,* enlivened by Waller's vocal comments. As Miss Brown complains, in battleship tones, about Waller's poor treatment of her, Tom hollers, "Tell these fools anything, but tell me the truth!" At the end of a verse blaming Waller for "spendin' all my money/And havin' yourself a ball," Tom declares: "Baby, I was *born* ballin', and I'm gon' ball the rest of my life." Miss Brown sings about visiting a fortune-teller and having the seer tell her that "all you wanted was my gold," to which Tom replies: "She was right—how'd she know?" The complete catalog of his roguery brings forth two immortal Wallerisms: "Beef to me, mama, beef to me—I don't like pork no-how," and a final, definitive dismissal, "Suffer, suffer, excess baggage, suffer!"

In the film, this performance brings him applause from the ringside table of the troupe, of which Robinson, Miss Horne, and a "bad guy" dancer and producer with romantic intentions toward swan Lena are members. Waller is urged to sing another tune as an audition; he responds with yet another reading of *Ain't Misbehavin',* after which Miss Horne opines: "Gee, he'd be great in the show!" Surprise, surprise—Tom is hired.

Waller does not appear again in the movie as an entertainer, but he has a shining moment with his most famous one-liner. In the previous scene, the bad guy, an egotistical sort, is dancing a production number, unaware that Robinson is behind him, dancing up twice a storm. The bad guy believes the ovation to be his and is furious when he finds out about Robinson's trick. He confronts Bojangles and insults him, throwing in a threat to stay away from Miss Horne. Robinson socks the bum on the jaw and lays him out cold, then leaves the dressing room. The offender is stretched on the floor when Waller happens by. In a little diamond of timing, Tom stops, looks, looks again, smiles benignly, delicately raises his eyebrows, tilts his head, wags it, gazes down at the cold-cocked baddie, and murmurs: "Well, well, well. One never knows, do one?"

Perfection.

The film was widely reviewed. *Time* magazine, which had run a feature piece on Waller a few months before, cited him as one of the treasures of the movie.

Kirkeby, diligently looking for ways to make the most of a Waller appearance, took the *Stormy Weather* opportunity to garner some extra money for his client. The producers had stipulated that Tom should perform *Ain't Misbehavin'* and had allowed for a comedy number to be shot *(That Ain't Right)*, but Kirkeby suggested that an original Waller tune be included. In this he had the collaboration of the associate producer, Irving Mills, the music publisher to whom Waller had sold his most valuable copyrights in 1929 for a piddling sum. *Moppin' and Boppin'* was quickly cooked up; it was not particularly distinguished, but Mills paid a few hundred dollars as a cash advance.

Though Waller was less prolific as a composer after 1934, when most of the material he performed was assigned to him by Victor, he still occasionally produced some charming tunes, two of which were *The Jitterbug Waltz* and *Honey Hush*. A "jitterbug" in "swing era" slang was a dance maniac, comparable to disco thrashers today. It was typical of the later Waller that he combined a contemporary social fad with the grace of light classical music, as if to mock the former and show the flexibility of the latter. The tune remains as a good-natured joke about a departed species.

The mood for composition struck Waller at hours which were odd to everyone but himself. Since his early touring days of the 1920s, he had found it difficult to sleep in strange towns, and he customarily stayed up until dawn. In the later stages of his career, he could afford to have company until the sun rose, usually his chauffeur or valet. Kirkeby's phone rang one morning, with Tom on the line asking, "Are you up?"

"Of course I am," Kirkeby snapped back. "Can't you hear me having my breakfast in bed?"

"Now, don't get mad, Mr. Kirkeby. I was just walking around in the park, and the birds were singing so pretty that they sang me a tune, and I want to get it down on paper before it does like a bird and flies away from me."

Kirkeby mumbled agreement—he respected Waller's creative urges if not Tom's body clock. The two men met and, sipping sherry, worked out the melody. Lacking a title, Kirkeby said, "Remember when we were sailing to England and that lady kept yammering at you and you said something to shut her up? What was it you said?"

"I told her, 'Honey, hush.'"

"That's our title."

Happy and satisfied, Waller ran a few chord sequences of his new melody, tossed down the last of the sherry, and went to bed.

Kirkeby, used to making quick moves on his client's behalf, also had long-range plans for Tom, and while *Stormy Weather* was shooting he received word from New York that negotiations he had been conducting by telegram and telephone had come good. Richard Kollmar, the producer for a proposed Broadway musical to be titled *Early to Bed,* agreed to have Waller in the cast. Kirkeby and Waller went to New York for face-to-face meetings, where Waller turned on his overwhelming charm. It was intended that Tom should act, play, and sing in the musical, and Kollmar gave a general description of the character Waller would essay. Then Kollmar mentioned that a composer was still being sought for the score. Kirkeby leaped in: Why should Kollmar look further? The man who wrote such tunes as Tom had, and still could, was sitting in front of him. Kollmar looked at Tom, whose face was already agleam at the prospect, and the Waller gleam could transform tundra into slush. Kollmar agreed.

There only remained to secure the approval of the man who was writing the lyrics and the book for the show, George F. Marion, Jr. A hot phone call was placed to Hollywood; Marion's consent was delighted and immediate. The astute Kirkeby mentioned an advance and Kollmar wrote a check for $1,000.

Through the late winter and early spring, Waller composed melodies to Marion's lyrics. All seemed to be going splendidly. Then one night there came another slightly dreadful Waller

phone call: Tom was sloshed, and he woozily informed Kirkeby
that the advance money was gone, that he had spoken to Kollmar and asked for another thousand, in return for which Tom
would sell his royalties from the score. Kirkeby told Waller not
to worry and to get some sleep. He said the same thing to Kollmar, who frantically phoned a few minutes later. Waller had
not completed the last two numbers assigned, and the show was
nearing dress rehearsal. Kirkeby calmed Kollmar by telling him
the truth: that Tom was much in the cups, that he didn't mean
what he said, that he would sleep such hasty words off, that he
would deliver the two songs on time, and that—for the comfort
of all concerned—it would be best to forget about Tom's taking
an acting role in the show. Kirkeby recommended the morning
after as a cure for all their ills, and sure enough, when the morning came, all was cured. Tom seldom took leave of his senses for
more than a day at a time.

The score was completed shortly thereafter, with Tom composing some of his most persuasive melodies. He was, in a sense,
taking on a new type of assignment. Though he had composed
for the Connie's Inn floor shows in the 1920s, those productions
were not full-blown musical comedy presentations, simply collec-
tions of songs interspersed with comedy routines. But the Broadway musical imposed a certain form on the score; the music had
to aid, develop, and complement the dramatic situation. Waller
quickly grasped the form and easily mastered it. His assignment
was not only immensely pleasing to him; it also carried a prestige that he welcomed. The Broadway theater in those days still
had, and deserved, a special and honored reputation: Broadway
was not only big-time, it was classy; and the composer of the
score for a hit show would move in the theater industry's upper
circles. Tom would be a candidate for the elite.

He was fortunate in that George F. Marion, Jr., was a literate
and worldly lyricist. Marion had spent most of his career as a
screenplay writer in Hollywood, and was one of five writers—the
theater's king of acerbic comedy, George S. Kaufman, among
them—who contributed to the script for *Million Dollar Legs*, a
1932 production starring W. C. Fields, which is still a hilariously
dizzy piece, with an outer-limits, Dada type of humor. Fields is

the president of a mythical country called Klopstockia, in which the succession to the presidency is determined not by popular election but by an Indian wrestle between the incumbent and the challenger. The president's daughter falls in love with a visiting American brush salesman. She hands him a parchment on which are written the words of *Oog Floogle Gloog,* the traditional Klopstockian courtship song. Feeling the parchment, the salesman asks: "What this made of?" and the maiden replies, "My grandfather." In another scene, the president's political rival entices the salesman to the den of the hussy and temptress, Mata Macree, played by Lyda Roberti, who goes through a seven-veils dance which fails to arouse the dumbo Yank. The oily political rival demands of her, "Can't you do anything else?" Macree shakes her head: "Not in public."

Marion's script for *Early to Bed* concerned the doings at a bordello disguised as a ladies' academy of higher learning on the island of Martinique. The girls in the chorus line were specially picked for their faces and legs and such zones of pelt as could be shown or inferred without the cops closing the show. The script's cheerful, cosmopolitan attitude toward whoring was manifest in the song titles and lyrics: *There's Yes in the Air, This Is So Nice (It Must be Illegal), There's a Man in My Life,* and *Slightly Less than Wonderful:*

> I think I'm on the brink of buying you mink
> To drag on the ground,
> A wrap around you when you slink.
>
> Within me elemental forces surge;
> Are you allergic to the basic urge?
> Must I, with deep regret, let etiquette guide me yet?
> And say to you politely: "Dear, you're only slightly
> Less than wonderful"?
>
> . . . .
>
> There's a man in my life responsible for
> The kind of a life I lead;
> He's the talk of my heart;
> When thoughts of him start
> I find myself a-tremble

Like a wind blown reed.
To one who never met him
This might seem extreme.
Still his charms can make me
Lay me down and dream.
Every plan in my life,
Each song in my soul
Has one unattainable goal:
The man in my life.

. . . .

This is so nice it must be illegal,
Meeting you once more.
Feeling so good, it could be against the law.
This is an age that curbs all our pleasures,
Who knows what's in store?
This is so nice there must be a hidden flaw.
You're so broad of shoulder
I know that, young and older,
All those dames fall in flocks;
Knowing your attractions
Congress may take actions
And keep you underground at Fort Knox.
Quick let us kiss, before it's [forbidden]
It could happen here[35];
This is so nice
It must be illicit, dear.

By May the show was on its tryout engagements. Joey Nash,
the sometime saxophonist turned singer whom Waller had be-
friended, remembered an ugly and unhappy incident:

Fats called me from New York, told me he was leaving for
Boston and to meet him early the next morning. . . . It wasn't the
time of day a musician would flip for joy but he was charged
with happiness with his *Early to Bed* tunes. He simply had to

---

[35]"It could happen here" refers to the title of a Sinclair Lewis novel of the
late 1930s, *It Can't Happen Here*, in which an American Hitler comes to
power.

play the score for me, without delay, right then and there. . . .
Waller spied a bar a few paces down the street and in a few
moments a dour bartender was asked if there was a piano in the
establishment. The back room had an abused, out of tune upright, an old box, its keyboard tattooed with cigar and cigarette
burns. Waller threw his coat and tie on a chair and started a run
down of the show's melodies. The customers out front were few,
so there was quiet. He was excited about every song, stopping to
repeat, again and again, phrases and chords he particularly fan-
cied. . . . *Early to Bed* was a triumph for Fats; every song was a
gem.

He told me he was busy the rest of the day with newspaper
interviews, radio appearances and a round of cocktail parties
given by the financial backers of the show and that he would see
me the following day for lunch.

Late that night I received a phone call from Fats. I had never
heard him so depressed. Would I take a cab over to his hotel? As
I entered the beatup lobby with its battered and ancient chairs
and faded, ink stained, moth eaten rug, I knew I was in a flop
joint. An aged, palsied clerk told me to walk up three flights. His
dismal room was the size of an iron lung. Overhead, banging
steam pipes hammered out a Morse code rhythm. A drab,
patched bed spread and a rust-stained wash basin hit my eyes.
Flapping in the breeze, a finger-smeared yellow window shade
hovered over Waller's chair.

Gone was the smiling face I had seen that morning. He was
unhappy, deeply humiliated. Briefly, he told me that after the
newpaper and radio interviews and the cocktail parties he went to
the hotel where the cast of *Early to Bed* were staying while in
Boston. The reservation clerk took one look at Fats and quickly
told him he didn't have a vacancy. Waller told him that he had
wired for a room reservation from New York. The clerk looked
him in the eye and brusquely said he never received the telegram.
Fats telephoned hotel after hotel and when they heard his name
they said they were very sorry but they were just jammed to capacity. Though his name was prominently displayed in the local
newspaper advertisements as the composer of *Early to Bed* and
MUSIC BY FATS WALLER was emblazoned in lights on the
Schubert Theatre marquee, this internationally acclaimed artist
was denied a decent place to live. Scornfully, he told me that the
hotel where he was an honored guest at a posh cocktail party

that afternoon, attended by some of the city's most prominent
people, later that day refused him a room. Fats remarked that in
his three trips to Europe, appearing in England, Scotland,
France, Sweden, Norway and Denmark he had received the red
carpet "proud to have you" treatment. But here in Boston,
U. S. A., it was a sad and different story.

Waller, according to Nash, left Boston that night to return to
the comfort and security of Harlem.

Yet even such painful incidents didn't affect the Waller resil-
iency for too long. The show did good business in Boston and
opened in New York on Thursday, June 17, 1943. Lewis Nichols, drama reviewer for the *New York Times,* found fault with
the show but none with Waller:

Since musical comedies not infrequently offer mixed blessings,
"Early to Bed," which opened last evening at the Broadhurst, is
long on body and short on mind. It undoubtedly has the most
beautiful chorus in the land, and its costumes and designs definitely are pre-priority[36], but it also has one of the most tedious
books on record. A suspicion exists this morning that on the
whole it is for those who take their musical comedy by eye rather
than ear, and an audience seeking brightness, sparkle and humor
may not find "Early to Bed" to its taste. But since it is summer,
say it is a summer musical and let it get by on that. . . .

To get over the negative and to the girls as quickly as possible,
the book as contributed by George Marion, Jr., is, to all intents
and purposes, frightful. The legend is of a house of dubious re-
pute on the island of Martinique, a house that pretends to be a
girls' school. There is one joke which can be made on that, and
Mr. Marion goes on making it long after the rains would have
washed out the original on the back alley fence. But possibly,
since musical comedy books hold no great reputation anyhow, it
doesn't matter as much as the tedium through long stretches of
the evening at the Broadhurst seem to suggest. . . .

Otherwise, life is pretty fair. The great "Fats" Waller has written the score for "Early to Bed," and has contributed a score that

---

[36] *Priority* was a wartime term having to do with government requisition of
any materials deemed necessary for military manufactures.

nicely serves its purposes. "There's a Man in My Life" is a pretty love song, and "Hi-De-Ho-High" is good Waller. "The Ladies Who Sing with a Band" is an excellent parody of what the title says it is, and there are several others including "Slightly Less than Wonderful" and "This !s So Nice." Don Walker, who knows about such things and understands the trumpets of Waller and the drums of Martinique, has done good orchestrations.

Early to Bed settled in for a comfortable and profitable run. Whether it would have been as successful without the wartime need for entertainment is a moot point, but in professional terms Tom Waller had scored big. In the pragmatic world of show business, where the bottom line of return on investment wars with the artistic and sentimental camaraderie of the gamble, Waller was the composer of the score of a hit show: he thus had what is known as "a credit," which made his talents more marketable and sought after. The prestige of *Early to Bed* could only increase his reputation as a star entertainer. The ease and speed with which he could deliver persuasive melodies would appeal to Broadway producers, who traditionally demand of composers that they yield sure-shot product on short notice, usually amid the bedlam of frantic revisions of the script shortly before the opening night of out-of-town previews. Who could rival Tom Waller for expertise and fast excellence?

Since 1934, when he began his recording career with the Rhythm and most of the tunes he performed were handed to him, Waller's composing career had been semidormant—with regular royalty payments and cash advances for recording sessions, there had been no need for him to put his talent on the quick-fry and come up with songs. But the discipline of composing for Broadway, where tunes had to be related to character development in the script, and where last-minute changes and crises were the rule, would confront him with a "deadline" mandate where his talent had to be quick as a whipcrack and as true as dreams. Tom Waller was uniquely qualified for such assignments.

There is no doubt that Waller was proud of his accomplishment with *Early to Bed,* and he lost no chance to remind audiences in clubs or on radio that he was the composer of a Broadway hit. He played selections from the score—and sang the lyrics carefully—everywhere he was booked. Both he and Kirkeby were frustrated by the American Federation of Musicians, continuing squabble with record companies over base wages; it meant that Waller couldn't record songs from the score to plug himself and the show. Had the ban and wartime "priorities" not been in effect Victor might have issued another Waller album[37] to tie in with the show and to promote one of its bestselling artists. It is tempting to imagine how Waller and the Rhythm (or whatever musicians he might have assembled for the date) would have presented his superior melodies in a jazz setting, especially since most of the score consisted of ballads—and when Waller sang a ballad with shy feeling, he suggested a hurt and secret heart that surprised and captured the listener, as *I'm Gonna Sit Right Down and Write Myself a Letter* had in 1935.

The success of *Early to Bed* kept Waller rolling along even more ebulliently than ever, and brought him renewed press attention. A rave major article in the *New York Times,* written by Murray Schumach, was published in August 1943.

> If Walt Disney ever decides to animate a volcano that erupts laughter and music let him just push a piano in front of Thomas (Fats) Waller and set up the drawing board. It doesn't have to be much of a piano, either. The one Fats worked out on the other day at the Broadhurst Theatre could have done with a little tuning. Yet for nearly two hours this Rabelais of the keyboard put on one of the best shows in town. He clowned, sang, bellowed; bounced around like a man possessed; made the piano talk in a dozen tongues.
>
> It was supposed to have been an interview with the composer of the score for "Early to Bed." But interviewing Mr. Waller is a bit like asking questions of Niagara Falls—inane and almost blasphemous. There is nothing to do but hang onto your seat and be grateful for eyes and ears. For he is an explosive and uninhibited zany whose mind is a musical warehouse. And he loves to play. One minute his sausagelike fingers pat out "Honeysuckle Rose,"

---

[37]An "album" in 1940s terms was a collection of 78-rpm singles gathered into a package, the package being called a "set."

and the next minute he is laughing like jelly as he tells how his father fanned him for "livening up" a hymn on the organ during church services. And through it all, those exuberant expletives like "bullllAM," and "whUmph"; and that lopsided grin and contagious chuckle, as natural and warming as a child's, with that same hint of sly coyness.

One thing the maestro of the bistro made clear—his musical credo. Concentrate on the melody. If it's good you don't have to shoot it out of a cannon. This maxim explains why, though he is one of the country's greatest jazz pianists and composers—he has written or collaborated on 360 songs—he dislikes most jazz turned out by name bands today; has an aversion for boogie-woogie; and he becomes really angry about the practice of making swing arrangements of the classics.

Waller spoke about his childhood, including his father's desire that he prepare himself for the ministry.

. . . He gestured as though to say: "Look at me. Can you imagine me as a minister!" He looked anything but a man of the cloth in a screaming blue shirt, multicolored tie, two-tone suit and Alpine hat. His foot began beating a slow rhythm and his husky voice gave out with "Praise God from whom all blessings flow"—in Waller tempo. "That's the way I played it on the organ when I was 9 years old and my father decided I wasn't cut out for the ministry."

Fats was tinkering with the piano and organ before he was 6. Yet it wasn't until five years later that he learned to read music. From then on studies didn't matter. He quit high school because he couldn't get enough music. Also he got too much algebra. "How I hated algebra," he exploded. "X means Q and Q means X and all that sort of stuff. I never knew what it was all about." So when he was 15 he left school for a job playing an organ in a Harlem movie for $23 a week. In a few months he went to another movie at the same job, paying $45 a week. How he lost that job is genuine Wallerania.

"That was during the silent movie days," he explained, "and I used to bat out the accompaniment. Well, one day, there's William S. Hart and he's been plugged and it looks like he's a cold mackerel. Pretty sad stuff, eh? All set for 'Hearts and Flowers,' eh? But the next thing I know, I'm playing 'St. Louis Blues.'"[38]

Tom jumped from subject to subject during the interview, pausing for musical interludes. He expressed his admiration for Art Tatum, and played Tatum's arrangement of *Tea for Two.*

> "That's music," he said after he had finished. "Subdued and not blatant. None of this boogie-woogie stuff that's just monotonous. Boogie-woogie is all right if you want to beat your brains out for five minutes. But for more than that you got to have melody. Jimmy Johnson taught me that. You got to hang onto the melody and never let it get boresome." . . .
>
> Not only does Fats like and understand the classics but the classical composers think highly of his musicianship. Thus, when Fats gave a concert at Carnegie Hall last year, he used Sergei Rachmaninoff's piano—at the latter's insistence. "Rachmaninoff," says Fats, "was my friend."

Waller continued to tour as a solo act, and to appear at many servicemen's entertainments, as well as guest on radio broadcasts. In late September he was called into the Victor studios for what was to be his last recording date, a series of thirteen sides for "V-disk" release to the Armed Forces Radio Network and USO clubs (the "V" stood for "Victory"). Waller was especially exuberant on the date, happy to be back in the recording studio, delighted to play four selections from *Early to Bed,* and his warmth to the fighting men radiated far beyond the microphone.

"Hiya, fellas! This is little Fats Waller, my mother's 285 pounds of jam, jive, and *everythin'.* They got me down here on the V-disk mess this afternoon, so watch out! Here 'tis! Latch on!"

The first selection was the inevitable *Ain't Misbehavin'.* It was

---

[38]There were several versions of this anecdote, depending on who was doing the telling. One variant had Bill "Count" Basie, whom Waller taught to play the organ while at the Lafayette Theatre, watching the screen aghast at a newsreel showing the burial of a French World War I general while Tom played *Squeeze Me.*

followed by an extended and hilarious version of *Two Sleepy People*. "And *now* . . . something soft, something quiet, *very* sentimental—*Two Sloppy*—no—*Two Sleepy People*—I always get that 'slop' and 'sleep' mixed up. Loook out!"

Waller plays a long piano introduction to his vocal—half-romantic, half-flowery—interspersed with spoken asides to the troops. "Glamour music, ya know, boys?" he drawls after a seductive passage, and then "Get this—get this," preparing his listeners for a keyboard run and then congratulating himself: "That's all right, ain't it?" At another point he confides: "Somethin's *ticklin'* me; I dunno what it is . . . maybe some Scotch I had last night." He plays a curlicue figure and guffaws: "Isn't that *cute?* Yaaaaas." As he nears the resolution of the bridge of the tune he advises, "Here we go up the hill," plays an ascending figure, and then conducts the audience on a descending figure: "Down the hill, yaaaas." As he approaches the vocal he hollers: "I wonder what Paul Robeson's doing—he should be down here on this V-disk business today."

Waller loads the lyrics about a newlywed couple cozying up, "too much in love to say goodnight," with a couple of erotic wisecracks. After the line "Do you remember the reason why we married in the fall?" Waller adds, "Yes—we had a shotgun wedding," and on the line "To rent this little nest and get a piece of rest," he emphasizes *"piece* of" and inserts a slight pause before finishing the lyric.

Next Waller presented *There's a Man [Girl] in My Life, Slightly Less than Wonderful, This Is So Nice (It Must Be Illegal),* and *Martinique:*

"Now, boys, I'm gonna give you a couple of tunes from my show, *Early to Bed* . . . a *fine* show on Broadway that . . . pays my backhouse dues, you know? I can't kid no more, but hold everything—here 'tis!"

Waller's performance of his show numbers is relatively straight, except for a fluffed line in *This Is So Nice* where he was thrown off by a female crony in the background unexpectedly singing harmony and by distant mumbles and giggles from other guests in the studio. During the piano introduction to *There's a Gal in My Life* he interjects, "Oh, what a half pint would do

right now!" (presumably he had just finished one), and he made
some giddy insertions into the lyrics:

> I find myself a-tremble like a wind-blown reed . . .
>> ["You know what a *reed* is—that's somethin' they play on a
>> saxophone—very stale."]
> . . . Responsible for the kind of a life I lead . . .
>> ["Yaaas, she led me on—I'se like a big, sad sap sucker . . ."]
> . . . each scheme in my soul has one unattainable goal
>> ["Yas! The jackpot!"]
> The girl in my life.

Waller closed his selections with the *Martinique* beguine, part
of *There's Yes in the Air*, the first-act finale which the *New York
Times* commended as the highlight of *Early to Bed*.

Waller was so concerned about entertaining the troops who
would be listening to his V-disk session that he even condes-
cended to play boogie-woogie on *Waller Jive*, because he knew
the soldiers liked the stuff, but it was a brief demonstration.
Immediately after, he played *Hallelujah!* by Vincent Youmans,
announcing the name of the composer, whom he admired. Youmans had written the score for *No, No, Nannette*, a smash musical of the 1920s, as well as the brilliant but unsuccessful *Great
Day!* Waller's interpretation of *Hallelujah!* included frequent references to classical composers.

Reefer Song (If You're a Viper), written by the jazz violinist
Stuff Smith, and *That's What the Bird Said to Me*, a mildly
vulgar joke tune, were—for obvious reasons—never released on
V-disks, but the test pressings of the recordings later found their
way onto a "pirate" label, appropriately named Jolly Roger, and
this glimpse of Waller as the hair-down, necktie-off, slightly
"dirty" entertainer became something of a collector's item.
Reefer Song ("I dreamed about a reefer five foot long") was a
funny and clever ditty about the delights of marijuana and its
effects on the viper (smoker), and it featured some yahoo Waller
comments ("Oh, darlin', I didn't know you *cared*—better nix it
on the sidelines; my wife's in here tonight—and she don't vipe,
either") plus a lip-smack imitation of a viper pulling too hard on

a reefer. But it is perhaps most notable for Waller's spoken introduction:

> Hey, cats! It's four o'clock in the mornin'. I just left the V-disk studios. Here we are in *Harlem*. Everybody's here except the police—and they'll be here *any* minute. It's high time! So latch on to this song. . . .

Waller finished the session with three organ solos: the superb *Sometimes I Feel like a Motherless Child;* Duke Ellington's *Solitude,* a companion piece in mood to the spiritual; and *Bouncin' on a V-Disk,* which was bouncy enough, but which Waller seemed to be playing with technique and little else—it is a fair bet that he had used up most of his remaining emotion on *Motherless Child* and *Solitude.* He had cut thirteen sides in a day—a substantial amount for any musician who gave as much of himself as Waller customarily did—but there was a special incentive for him in knowing that these records would be played for soldiers fighting the good fight.

Once done with the session, Tom resumed his schedule of club work, radio guest shots, and troop entertainments.

Waller was booked into the Zanzibar Room in Los Angeles for a two-week run. At first, there was some trouble about the piano. Waller's contracts specified that he be provided with a fine-tuned Steinway concert grand. Kirkeby went to the club before opening night, and saw that the instrument available would not please Waller. Then, over his shoulder, he saw Waller walking through the door. Kirkeby hurriedly explained the details of the contract to the club owner, and advised him that Waller would walk out the door directly if a proper instrument wasn't provided. While the club manager was hastily agreeing, Waller sat down at the piano and played a few test chords. He scowled and stood up, saying, "Mr. Kirkeby, let's go home." But he was all smiles when Kirkeby announced that the club manager was sending Tom to the local Steinway dealer to pick out the piano of his choice. It was delivered that afternoon, and Waller happily began his run.

The Zanzibar Room was packed, with Waller at the top of the

bill, but unknown to Kirkeby, who knew how Waller suffered from heat (he had cancelled some appearances that summer in New York because of the traditionally ghastly Manhattan humidity), there was an air conditioner above and behind the piano.

Waller customarily protected himself on close, stuffy bandstands, where he worked up a sweat, by draping a handkerchief over his head, and then using it as a convenient excuse to go into *The Sheik of Araby* (a *Time* magazine article in 1943 showed him with a "doily" on his head, a glass in his hand, and a sweetly blotto expression on his face). But the air conditioning at the Zanzibar Room quickly led to a smashing attack of the flu.

Kirkeby wanted to take Waller to a hospital, but Tom refused, confining himself to his hotel bed. The manager brought in two doctors to keep tabs on the patient, and he watched carefully over Tom. After ten days the doctors said Tom could get up, and Kirkeby, still concerned, wanted Waller to do no more than was required of him, but Tom's illness had forced him to cancel an appearance on a radio program called *Colored, U. S. A.,* as well as a *Hollywood Canteen* program for soldiers. Waller insisted on honoring both commitments, as well as other, commercial commitments, plus going on with the long evenings of his run at the Zanzibar.

By the time his run at the club ended, Waller was utterly exhausted. A few days previously, an afternoon press party had been scheduled, and he was looking forward to it, so much so that the night before, while he was out drinking, he called Kirkeby every hour on the hour to remind him of the event. Came the day, and a bleary-eyed Tom was playing the piano and trying hard to stay awake at his party. Kirkeby, worried, told him that he truly needed sleep. Waller nodded agreement, stopped playing, crawled under the piano, and was out like a light.

Waller moved in a semiconscious state through the last three nights of his run at the Zanzibar, the final night being the most difficult. He was in such droopy shape that Kirkeby actually thought to offer him a cup of coffee, and Waller actually drank it.

Christmas was close on. Both Kirkeby and Waller looked forward to returning to New York for the holidays, and Kirkeby had made preparations that were almost military in their precision for getting Waller out of Los Angeles and on board the transcontinental train without his client's being waylaid by partygoers and carousing well-wishers. As soon as Tom's last set was finished, Kirkeby hustled him out through the kitchen, took him to his hotel, and left strict instructions that Tom's telephone was to be cut off until ten o'clock the next morning, when they were due to pack their bags and race to the railroad station.

They arrived at the station on time and found that a few West Coast friends had beaten them there so as to be able to wish them bon voyage. Waller's Hollywood tailor was also present, handing Tom a bill for six suits. Tom paid it, and he and Kirkeby boarded the Sante Fe.

Shortly after the train pulled out, Waller made a rare complaint, saying, "Oh, man, I just can't take much more of this." Kirkeby tried to perk Tom up by pointing out that, at long last, Tom's income was catching up with his outgo: "You'll never have to do one-nighters again."

While they were in the club car, a small mob of good-timers recognized Waller, and a miniparty began to get underway. Some of the revelers were brought into the sleeping compartment Waller and Kirkeby were sharing until at midnight the manager politely chased them out.

The next morning Tom elected to stay in bed and sleep the whole day—not an unusual practice for him—and Kirkeby did not see Tom until that evening, when he entered Tom's compartment and was hit by freezing air. The train was halfway across the continent, and the December winds were roaring across Kansas. "Yeah, Hawkins is sure out there tonight," Waller mumbled, referring to his friend, the tenor saxophonist Coleman Hawkins. Kirkeby got into bed.

It was about five o'clock in the morning when I woke and heard a choking sound coming from Fats' bed. Quickly I switched on the light and saw Fats . . . trembling all over. I jumped out of bed, and shaking him by the shoulder, called him to wake up. It seemed he was having a bad dream, but I couldn't wake him. Frantically I rang for the porter . . . but no porter was on hand. I ran back quickly to the club car, found the bar steward and we both rushed back to Fats. By the time we got back to the sleeper, our porter and several others were there gazing at Fats' motionless figure.

"Get a doctor quickly," I called, "and don't move this train until we do."

A doctor appeared very quickly, for he had been called to attend another passenger. In absolute silence, while we watched, the doctor moved his stethoscope about, tested for pulse, breathing and eyelids, and, after what seemed to me ages, looked up and quietly said, "This man is dead."

Thomas Wright "Fats" Waller, aged thirty-nine, was dead of influenzal bronchial pneumonia. He had never recovered completely from his attack of flu while playing the Zanzibar, and the violent temperature change from the warmth of Los Angeles to the furious blizzard screaming over the Kansas plains resulted in an ugly combination of influenza and bronchial pneumonia which the exhausted Waller could not withstand. The influenza produced liquid in his lungs, and the bronchial pneumonia hardened his lungs so that he could not receive air. He suffocated and drowned at the same time. When Kirkeby woke to Waller's "trembling" and "choking" he was witnessing the spasms and twitches of death; there was nothing Kirkeby or any doctor could have done to save the composer.

The dazed and pained Kirkeby spent the next two days dealing with phone calls and interviews from the national press, arranging for the body to be placed in a casket, and accompanying it on a train to New York.

Waller's funeral service was held at the Abyssinian Baptist Church. The attendees were Waller's friends and professional peers, white and black, while outside a crowd of thousands was bunched up for three blocks square. The Reverend Adam Clayton Powell, Jr., later to become a corrupt congressman and a disgrace to his people, delivered a rather tepid lay-to-rest eulogy. It is ironic that a Harlem boulevard has been named after the smarmy Powell but that no monument commemorates Waller's love for the community to which he returned so often for comfort and inspiration.

A picture of Waller's coffin being loaded onto the hearse appeared on the next morning's *Daily News* back cover, a space traditionally reserved for sports photos, which, with rare exceptions, are dislodged only by pictures of presidential elections and other national calamities.

Waller's body was taken to Fresh Pond Crematory where, by the terms of Waller's will (which Kirkeby had persuaded him to sign only the previous October), it met the requirements of the biblical dictum "ashes to ashes."

The newspaper obituary and funeral stories were of unusual length for the passing of a black man in 1943. The notices reflected not only Waller's stardom but the comradely charm that was uniquely his and would be so badly missed.

Waller continued to be newsworthy until May 1944. In February of that year his will reached probate: "Jazz King Left Wife Legal 3rd" and "Waller Will Cuts Widow" were the headlines of two stories revealing that Waller's first wife, Edith, received the minimum bequest permissible by law "for reasons that are fully known to her." The bitterness of his alimony experiences survived the grave. For a moment it looked as though Waller's last composition might also survive. "Woman's Memory Holds Only Copy of Waller's Last Song" described Mrs. Joyce Seamon, a Jamaican-born pianist with a degree from the Royal Academy of Music in London, who worked for Pan American Airways at La Guardia Airport. "Mrs. Seamon said she had heard Waller play his last composition, which she described as a delicate waltz. The music was never placed on paper but she hopes to meet the request of his manager and record it from memory." So far as is known, nothing came of the project.

Waller's death brought about a revival of interest in his teacher, patron, and musical father, James P. Johnson. A *Time* feature piece on Johnson appeared not long after Tom's passing. James P. had been one of the pallbearers, and for three days after hearing the awful news from Kansas City he had been unable to touch a piano. Later, discussing his artistic relationship with Waller, Johnson told the magazine:

I taught him how to groove, how to make it sweet—the strong
bass line he had dates from that time. He stuck pretty well to my
pattern—developed a lovely singing tone, a lyric, melodic expression. . . .

Johnson also mentioned another most important ingredient:

. . . and then, too, him being the son of a preacher, he had fervor.

16
The Call

"LIVE INTENSELY AND DIE SUDDENLY" was the motto of one of
the many Galahads to Winston Churchill's ravishing and sassy
mother, and the motto also held true for Waller's life. He had
spent it recklessly and brilliantly. But did he mean to leave it so
soon?

When it came to finances, Waller always believed that no matter how much money he spent and no matter how deep he was
in hock, there would still be cash enough, and more, just around
the corner. Did he feel the same about life?

Waller was a sensualist. He excluded from his life or tried to
avoid anything which did not offer the pleasures of the table, the
bottle, and the bed. His passion for music was complete, mysti-
cal, even erotic.

Yet he was a shrewd man, well versed in human experience
(what would now be called "street smarts"), and if he was sometimes foolish he was certainly not a fool. With the doctor's stern
warning about his drinking in 1942, and the memory of his
mother's diabetes, and the punishing schedules of his professional appearances, he must have known that he could not in-

definitely continue his habits and pace without some sort of comeuppance. Yet he continued, especially in the last years of his life, to ransack his energy and pillage his health. Given that an intelligent man knows he cannot overextend himself so carelessly without death calling in the loan, we are left with the question: Did Tom Waller deliberately burn himself out—did he seek to die?

A number of men and women who are larger than life dare death to claim them; their pleasure comes in the defiance. The death need not be physical: it can involve social or political ostracism, financial ruin, the wreck of a career. None of this applied to Tom Waller. He was not political—so far as is known, he never voted. As a black, he was forced to observe, avoid, or suffer under certain social taboos, but he managed to dodge most of them by staying close to Harlem. Despite financial emergencies, he was seldom destitute; he believed that money was for spending, whether he had it or not, and all his life he teetered cheerfully at the brink of bankruptcy. His career, by any standard, was artistically and commercially successful: he was loved not only by his peers but by an immense national audience; he was a star.

Some men and women who are larger than life leave clues as to when they expect to die, and why. They either forecast their death or place themselves in situations where they are likely to be carried off. The great actor John Barrymore, who, in the words of his biographer Gene Fowler, "did not become a serious alcoholic until he was fourteen," told a friend that he had made a vow to God that if his wife (Barrymore's third, and the one he loved most deeply) gave him a son he would stop drinking. His wife delivered a baby boy and called for her husband. Barrymore was off somewhere getting potted. When he sobered up and remembered his vow, he asked his friend, "I wonder what happens to a man who breaks a promise like that."

Ambrose Bierce, the savage and talented cynic, whose funeral wit produced classic short stories of horror and the finest naysaying epigrams in the English language *(The Devil's Dictionary)*, arranged a tour to Mexico in 1913 when that country was in the midst of a ferocious and barbaric civil war. Bierce wrote to acquaintances that "you may hear of me being stood against a wall and shot to rags. . . . to be a *gringo* in Mexico—ah! that is euthanasia."

What clues did Waller drop about his own passing?

Willie "The Lion" Smith recalled that he, Waller, and James P. Johnson

> used to argue about reincarnation. James P. believed in it. Fats didn't believe that a man's soul returned in any other form during a future era. It was Waller's wish that he be cremated and he was.

Eugene "Honeybear" Sedric, in an interview given two years after Waller's death, said:

> He was a great man. He lived every day. I heard him say that when he died the world would owe him nothing.

Sedric also stated of Waller that

> he often said that someday he might become a preacher and go out and give sermons with a big band behind him.

Ten years later, in another interview, Sedric reaffirmed that Waller was

> Very religious, very religious. He was a Bible student. I believe that had he lived his ambition was to have a big traveling religious show.

Kirkeby wrote:

> Outstanding in the memories of his bandsmen are countless times when, in the dressing-room between shows, Fats would read to them from the Bible . . . which he had read since childhood. . . . he could quote long passages and was adept at translating the Old Testament meanings into everyday terms. . . .
>
> Fats always insisted that his children went to Sunday School and, when asked why he didn't go himself, he said simply that he

didn't think the life he led in the entertainment world qualified
him for proper church attendance.

Bound up with Waller's respect for the dictates and challenges
of Christianity was another, deeper, and determining emotion
which Kirkeby recorded in the late 1940s:

> In our rare private moments together, Tom was an intelligent,
> religious person, capable of thoughtful expression; and invariably
> thoughts of his mother would become vocal. He never really got
> over the loss of his mother whom he idealized, and I have heard
> him many times cry: "Oh, if only my mother were here." In a
> moment of great emotion not long ago he composed a melody of
> great depth; one that really shook his soul, which he titled,
> *Where Has My Mother Gone?* Several lyrics with different titles
> were written, but none were accepted by Tom. None satisfied him
> nor adequately expressed the anguish of that melody.

It is certain that Waller's longing for his mother could only be
satisfied by meeting her in Heaven, and that he believed he
would. Passionate Christianity, especially the variant of southern
origins, has long been considered by northern urban intellectuals
to be the fantastic and vulgar goat dances of yokels, white and
black. But black Christianity, although it has attracted scalawags, flimflam experts and outright satyrs to the ministry, has
remained a powerful and cohesive social force among the black
population. When Edward Martin Waller and his bride Adeline
took the train to New York from Bermuda Hundred, Virginia,
at the turn of the century, the principal gift from their wedding
party was a Bible.

In his newspaper and radio interviews Fats Waller made frequent references to how he became a jazz musician: "They
stopped me from swingin' in church, so I had to swing outside."
He used to joke about how his father had wanted him to become a minister, and how he had been chastised when he slipped
a little syncopation into the playing of hymns at the frequent—
nay, relentless—Waller family home services. But Fats Waller's
favorite instrument was the organ, and his first keyboard instrument was the harmonium in his parents' house. His love affair

with the organ, which he had heard his mother play at church services, leads one to conclude that while the piano may have been his mistress, the organ was his wife. Waller's emotional hungers were as gargantuan as his appetite, and only the massive, total, infinite sound of the "God-box" could satisfy or assuage them. His recordings of spirituals were his most personal statements. On his final studio date, in 1943, the last recording he made was *Sometimes I Feel like a Motherless Child*, which he had been incapable of performing in London in 1939, when he broke down and sobbed. The companion piece in mood which he recorded at the same date was Duke Ellington's *Solitude*, which contains gospel sentiments.

Knowing that Waller's religious feeling was strong, knowing that on several occasions he had said that he might one day become a preacher—as his father had wished—and remembering that despite a doctor's warning about his health he was pushing himself unmercifully to entertain troops in a war which was popularly (and quite rightly) seen as being a crusade against an anti-Christian enemy, is it only speculation to say that Waller was hurrying to a death which, as a Christian, he did not see as the end of life but as the beginning of immortal life?

Certainly Waller's performances for the troops, and the generosity of his affection for them, qualified him as some sort of chaplain (he did not receive any fees for such performances), and he accepted nearly every request to give them. Waller felt it a Christian duty, as well as a pleasure, to give comfort and laughter to men who were going to experience deadly combat. (He could not have had any naive notions about the realities of war; his brother Robert, who had served with the great 369th Division in 1918, must have told him the facts of front-line life.)

It was an accident of history that the United States entered World War II at a moment when Waller's reckless and giddy habits were catching up with him. But his deliberate and willful exertions beyond what doctors and his common sense told him he was capable of sustaining without ruining his health do not appear to be an accident.

One of the accepted and familiar phenomena of passionate Christianity as manifested in the South is "the call," a moment when a man (or woman, or child) feels, senses, and is possessed by a personal union with Christ, and by a directive from Heaven to speak and act God's will on earth and to proselytize. It is an infinitely sweet moment, overpowering and commanding. It can come at any time, in any circumstances, and in any company, but the person who experiences it feels that he knows for certain what he has been placed on earth for, and his life is suddenly transformed into a mandate of bliss and duty.

While there is no evidence that Waller ever received "the call," and while his parents never claimed to have been more than devout Christians, Waller could not have been his parents' son, nor lived in Harlem, with its kaleidoscope of religious sects, many of them evangelical, without being aware of "the call."

Though Waller probably did not experience "the call," his dream of becoming a preacher giving sermons with a big band behind him would have brought him closer to his mother's memory and would have pleased his father's shadow. Like Winston Churchill, who adored his mother and kept finding excuses for his father's rejection of him, Waller might have been able, through his dream of preaching, to have resolved the emotional squeeze that bothered him all his life: how to make the transition from childhood to adulthood.

Thomas Wright Waller was never able to solve his dilemma, and much of his music and personality was a brave and resolutely carefree mask designed to hide a deep vulnerability. It is to his great credit that the weapon he chose to defend himself against his personal pain was public joy. Those of us who will see Heaven might well make the journey if only for the sure and certain hope that meeting this master musician and generous gentleman will be worth the price of admission.

Bibliography

Apel, Willi. *Harvard Dictionary of Music.* Cambridge, Massachusetts, 1969.

Asbury, Herbert. *The Gangs of New York.* New York, 1927.

ASCAP Biographical Dictionary, Third Edition. New York, 1966.

Blesh, Rudi. Liner notes to the album "The Original Dixieland Jazz Band," RCA Vintage, LPV-547, *circa* 1967.

Charters, Ann. *Nobody: The Story of Bert Williams.* New York, 1970.

Cooke, Roy. Liner notes to the record album "Young Fats at the Organ, Volume 1, 1926-1927." RCA (French pressing) 741.052.

Dance, Stanley. Liner notes to the record album "Young Louis: The Side Man," Decca DL 79233, *circa* 1967.

————. Liner notes to the record album "Fletcher Henderson: First Impressions, 1924-1931," Decca DL 79227, *circa* 1967.

Drotning, Phillip T. *Black Heroes in Our Nation's History*. New York, 1969.

Ellis, Edward Robb. *The Epic of New York City*. New York, 1966.

Ferguson, Blanche E. *Countee Cullen and the Negro Renaissance*. New York, 1966.

Fox, Charles. *Fats Waller*. Kings of Jazz Series. London, 1960; New York, 1961.

Hentoff, Nat and Nat Shapiro (editors). *Hear Me Talkin' to Ya: The Story of Jazz by the Men Who Made It*. New York, 1955.

Hoefer, George. Accompanying booklet to the 3-record album "The Sound of Harlem," Columbia C3L 33, *circa* 1964.

Kirkeby, W. T. (Ed), in collaboration with Duncan P. Scheidt and Sinclair Traill. *Ain't Misbehavin': The Story of Fats Waller*. New York, 1966.

Lipskin, Mike. Liner notes to the RCA Vintage record albums "34/35" (LPV-516); "Valentine Stomp" (LPV-525); "Fractious Fingering" (LPV-537); "Smashing Thirds" (LPV-550); and "African Ripples" (LPV-562), *circa* 1966-1968.

_____. Liner notes to the record album "The Undiscovered Fats Waller," Stanyan 10057, *circa* 1973.

Nash, Joey. Liner notes to the 2-record album "The Complete Fats Waller, Volume 1, 1934-1935" (RCA Bluebird AXM2-5511), 1976.

_____. "Memories of Fats Waller," *Jazz* magazine, January, 1966.

Smith, Willie "The Lion," with George Hoefer. *Music On My Mind: the Memoirs of an American Pianist*. New York, 1964.

Sudhalter, Richard M., and Evans, Philip R., with William Dean-Myatt. *Bix: Man and Legend*. New York, 1974.

Index

Abide with Me, 8, 67
Abyssinian Baptist Church (Harlem), 8,
    15, 162
Adrian's Tap Room, 90
African Ripples, 94
Ahlert, Fred, 103, 104
Ain't Misbehavin', 58, 76-77, 119, 131,
    145, 156
American Federation of Musicians, 140-
    41, 154
"Amos 'n' Andy," 95
Anderson, Eddie "Rochester," 129-35
Apollo Theatre (NYC), 72n, 96
Arlen, Harold, 109n
Armstrong, Louis, 7, 16-17, 30, 34, 44, 46-
    47, 51, 59, 60, 74, 94n
ASCAP, 3, 8, 107-8
A-Tisket, A-Tasket, 119
At the Darktown Strutters' Ball, 117
At the Moving Picture Ball, 52
Austin, Gene, 57, 83, 84
Autry, Gene, 8n
Autry, Herman, 94

Baby, Won't You Please Come Home?,"
    34
Bailey, Buster, 60
Baker, Josephine, 86
Banjo, 61n
Banks, Billy, 88
Bargy, Roy, 80n
Barker, Danny, 47
Barron's (NYC), 73
Barrymore, John, 12n, 166

Basie, "Count," 127, 156n
Bass saxophone, 90
Baxter, Warner, 106
Beale Street Blues, 67
Because of Once upon a Time, 100
Bechet, Sidney, 44
Beiderbecke, Bix, 18n, 53, 59, 60, 61-62,
    63, 70, 80n
Benny, Jack, 131n
Berlin, Irving, 41, 94
Big Butter and Egg Man, 52
Big John's Cafe (NYC), 74
Birmingham Blues, 36
Black and Blue, 22, 59-60, 76
Black Christianity, 16-17, 168, 169
Black neighborhoods (NYC), 12-14
Blake, Eubie, 6, 23n, 72
Blue Five, 81
Bond Street, 125
Boogie-woogie, 5, 6, 133, 155, 156, 158
Bop, 111n
Boston Blues, The, 42
Bouncin' on a V-Disk, 159
Boy in the Boat, The, 40, 42
Breakin' the Ice, 94, 101-2
Bricktop's (Paris), 86
Brill Building (NYC), 98
Brooks, Russell, 26, 27
Brooks, Wilson, 26-27
Brown, Ada, 145
Brown, Edmund "Mule," 74
Brunies, George, 52, 53, 81-82
Bryant, Freddy, 5
Buck, Gene, 8

Burr, Henry, 117

California Ramblers, 117
Cantor, Eddie, 22
Carlisle, Una Mae, 89-90
Carnegie Hall, 78, 135-39, 156
Carolina Shout, 27, 30, 34
Carter, Benny, 60, 63
Caruso, Enrico, 108
Casey, Al, 95, 96
CBS radio, 5, 91, 93, 98
Challis, Bill, 63
Chamber-music jazz, 61n
Charleston, The, 51
Chattanooga Choo Choo, 83n
Chelsea, 125-26
Chicago Loopers, The, 61, 62
Chitlin' circuit, 38, 39
Clef Club, 22
Columbia Records, 35n, 80, 82, 117
"Columbia Variety Hour," 93
Condon, Eddie, 48-49, 52, 56, 88, 135
Connie's Inn (NYC), 72-73, 74, 76-77, 108, 148
Copyright Law (1909), 3, 107-8
Correll, Charles, 95
Cottage in the Rain, 119
Cotton Club (NYC), 73
Crawford, Jesse, 69-70, 81
Crazy 'bout My Baby, 82, 84
Crazy Blues, 35, 83
Crosby, Bing, 96, 103
Custom recordings, 69

Daily Worker (Daily World), 138
Daisy Chain, 74
Dallas Blues, 53
Davis, Joe, 81
Davis, Leonard, 52
Deep River Boys, The, 117n
Depression, 79-80, 81
Dial, Harry, 101
D Major Blues, 63
Donaldson, Walter, 74
Don't Try Your Jive on Me, 119
Dorsey, Tommy and Jimmy, 117
Do What You Did Last Night, 109n
Downes, Marie, 25

Draggin' My Heart Around, 2
Dream Man, 94
Du Bois, W. E. B., 75
Duncan, Hank, 104-5

Early to Bed, 9, 147-54, 157
Edmund's Cellar (NYC), 74
Edwards, Cliff "Ukulele Ike," 83, 84
Edwards, James, 144
Ellington, Duke, 14, 52, 59-60, 68, 73, 97
Emperor Jones, The, 143
Europe, James Reese, 22, 23

Fascination, 42
Fat Man's Cafe, The (NYC), 74
Fats Waller & His Rhythm, 5, 93-94, 95-96, 97, 98, 100-102, 103-4, 129
"Fats Waller's Rhythm Club," 88-90, 93
Feather, Leonard, 118, 119
Fields, W. C., 21, 22, 148-49
Fitzgerald, Ella, 119
Flat Foot Floogie, 118-19
Flat Tire Papa, Mama's Gonna Give Him Air, 3, 107-9
Forsythe, Reginald, 85, 94, 124
Four Wanderers, The, 52
Fox Terminal Theatre (Newark), 81

Gaines, "Captain" George, 58
Gant, Willie, 6
Garvey, Marcus, 75
Gee, Baby, Ain't I Good to You, 51
Geechee, 51
Gennett Records, 80
Georgia Bo-Bo, 44
Gershwin, George, 37-38, 40-41, 91
Get Some Cash for Your Trash, 3, 141
Gladyse, 94
Go Down, Moses, 119
Godowsky, Leopold, 41, 91
Gold record, 83n
Goodman, Benny, 53, 81, 135-36, 138
Gophers, 73
Gosden, Freeman, 95
Gould, Walter "One Leg Shadow," 74
Grace, "Sweet Daddy," 75
Grappelli, Stephane, 61n
Greenwich Village (NYC), 11

Gulf Coast Blues, 34

Hall, Adelaide, 110, 120
Hallelujah!, 158
Hammond, John, 85, 87, 88, 136
Hampton, Lionel, 138
Handy, W. C., 135
Hardin, Lil, 44
Hardwick, Otto, 52
Harlem (NYC), 8, 11, 12-14, 15, 38, 71-75, 110, 162-63
Harlem Fuss, 49
Harmonium, 66, 67
Harper, Leonard, 77
Harrison, Jimmy, 60
Hart, William S., 155
Hatch, Ike, 118
Hatchett, Edith, 25, 36, 55-56, 163
Have a Little Dream on Me, 94, 99
Have It Ready, 63-64
Hawkins, Coleman, 7, 60, 90, 161
Hell's Kitchen (NYC), 12
Henderson, Fletcher, 4, 51, 60-61, 63-64, 74, 84, 90-91
Henderson, Leora, 61, 63
Hines, Earl, 4, 7, 59, 69, 111
His Master's Voice, 118
Hog Maw Stomp, 66
Home to Harlem, 75
Honey Hush, 146-47
Honeysuckle Rose, 58, 94, 116
Hooray for Love, 104
Hope-Jones, Robert, 66
Horne, Lena, 144-46
Horowitz, Vladimir, 136
Hot Chocolates, 76, 77
Hot Five Band, 44
Hot Mustard, 63-64
How Can You Face Me?, 98
Hughes, Langston, 75
Hunter, Alberta, 67
Hurtig & Seamon's Theatre (NYC), 72n, 96

I Ain't Got Nobody, 108
I Believe in Miracles, 100
I Can't Give You Anything but Love, 120
I Cried for You, 83

If I Had You, 44
I Got Rhythm, 104-5
I'll Be Glad When You're Dead, You Rascal You, 53
I'm Crazy about My Baby, 53
I'm Going to See My Ma, 67
I'm Goin' Huntin', 44
I'm Gonna Sit Right Down and Write Myself a Letter, 103, 154
Immerman, Connie and George, 71-72
I'm More than Satisfied, 61-62
In a Mist, 60, 61
I Need Someone like You, 52
In Harlem's Araby, 44
I've Got My Fingers Crossed, 104
I Wish I Could Shimmie Like My Sister Kate, 34
I Would Do Anything for You, 88

Jack the Bear, 5
Jean Goldkette Orchestra, 52, 60, 63
Jitterbug Waltz, The, 146
Johnson, Henry, 22-24
Johnson, James P.,
    Charleston, 5, 51
    compositions, 75-76, 78, 93
    nickname, 33
    recording, 35
    Smith and, 33, 34, 37, 167
    stride music, 5, 6, 26, 29-31
    Tatum and, 110
    Waller and, 26, 27, 29-31, 32-34, 39-40, 42, 66, 74, 111, 121, 156, 163-64
Johnson, Lillian Mae, 33, 34
Joint Is Jumpin', The, 9, 39
Jolly Roger, 158
Joplin, Mrs. Lottie, 74
Joplin, Scott, 19, 26, 30, 66
Julian, "Colonel" Herbert Fauntleroy, 75
June Night, 83
Jungle Jamboree, 59, 97
"Jungles, The" (NYC), 11, 12, 15

Keep Shufflin', 73, 75
King of Burlesque, 106, 107
Kirkeby, W. T. (Ed), 6, 7, 8, 54, 113, 115, 116-17, 118, 119, 124-25, 127-29, 139, 141, 146-48, 154, 159-63, 167

Koehler, Ted, 107
Kollmar, Richard, 9, 147-48
Krupa, Gene, 52, 135
Kyle, Billy, 111, 112

Labba, Abba, 5
Lafayette Theatre (NYC), 66, 72, 73, 75, 155-56
Lang, Eddie, 61
La Rumba (Paris), 86
Leadbelly, 30
Lee, Canada, 8, 18, 143-44
Lemke, Johannes, 136
Levant, Oscar, 136
Lewis, Ted, 52, 53, 81
Lillie's Chicken Shack (NYC), 74
Lil's Hot Shots, 44
Lincoln Theatre (NYC), 25, 27, 66, 72
Lipskin, Mike, 36
Livery Stable Blues, 83, 117
Load of Coal, 76
London Suite, 125-26, 135
Lookin' Good but Feelin' Bad, 52
Louisiana Fairy Tale, 100-101
Lyon & Healy, 68

McDaniel, Hattie, 144
MacDonnell, Leslie, 117-18
McHugh, Jimmy, 107
McKay, Claude, 75
McKinney's Cotton Pickers, 51-52, 84
Madden, Owney "The Killer," 73
Maines, Captain George, 81
Mandy, 94, 101
Marion, George F., Jr., 147, 148, 149, 152
Martin, Sara, 35, 36n
Martinique, 157, 158
Mason, Billy, 116
Mean Old Bed Bug Blues, 88
Messin' Around with the Blues, 66
Miller, Glenn, 83n
Million Dollar Legs, 148-49
Mills, Irving, 146
Minor Drag, The, 49
Minton's (NYC), 111n
Mitropoulos, Dimitri, 139-40
Monk, Thelonious, 111-12
Moonlight Sonata (film), 19n

"Moon River," 89
Moppin' and Boppin', 146
Morris, Thomas, 51
Morris' Hot Babies, 51, 84
Morton, Ferdinand La Menthe "Jelly Roll," 74, 80, 84
Mosley, Snub, 104
Mullins, Mazie, 25
Murray, Don, 52-53
Muscle Shoals Blues, 36
Musicians' Union, 113
Music, Maestro, Music, 119
My Blue Heaven, 57, 74, 83
My Fate Is in Your Hands, 57-58, 76, 131n
My Military Man, 109n

Nash, Joey, 97-98, 133, 150-52
NBC, 113, 129
Near beer, 73n
Nesbitt, Evelyn, 12n
New Orleans Rhythm Kings, 52, 53, 81-82
New York, New York, 11. See also Harlem
Nichols, Red, 61, 117
Night Wind, 100
Nobody, 22
Noodling, 61

Oh, Mr. Mitchell, 109n
Okeh Records, 35, 36, 44
Old Pal, Why Don't You Answer Me?, 117
135th Street, 40
Onyx Club (NYC), 111
Organ, 65-67
Original Dixieland Jazz Band, 83-84, 117
Ory, Edward "Kid," 44

Paderewski, Ignace, 19
Page, Oran "Hot Lips," 111n, 135
Paine, Bennie, 80
Paley, William S., 91, 93
Panassie, Hughes, 87, 119
Panpipe, 65
"Paramount on Parade," 81
Paramount Records, 80

Paramount Theatre (NYC), 70n, 81
Paris, France, 85-86
Payton, E. Phillip, 13
Peer, Ralph, 36
Pent Up in a Penthouse, 119
Perfect Records, 80, 84
Performers and Entertainers Club (NYC), 74
Pershing, General John J., 23
Piano, 5, 18, 31, 159
Piccadilly, 125
Pickett, Jess, 5
Please Take Me Out of Jail, 51
Pod & Jerry's (NYC), 74
Ponce, Phil, 88, 89, 93, 104, 113
Porgy and Bess, 40
Porter's Love Song to a Chambermaid, A, 93-94
Powell, Adam Clayton, 8, 162

QRS piano roll company, 31, 34
Quintet of the Hot Club of France, 61n

Race records, 35
Rachmaninoff, Sergei, 156
Radio, 80-81
"Radio Roundup," 81
Ragtime, 5, 6, 26
Razaf, Andy, 57, 59, 76, 93, 98, 131n
RCA Victor, 5, 69. *See also* Victor Records
Record industry, 79-80, 83, 84, 141
Recording Industry Association of America (RIAA), 83n
Red Hot Peppers, 84
Redman, Don, 51
Red Nichols and His Five Pennies, 61, 123
Reefer Song, 158-59
Reinhardt, Django, 61n
Rent parties, 38-40
Reuben's (NYC), 74
Rhapsody in Blue, 41, 44
Rhythm Club (NYC), 74
"Rhythm Club" (radio program). *See* Fats Waller's Rhythm Club
Robbins, Jack, 44
Roberts, Charles Luckyeth, 6, 18

Robeson, Paul, 143
Robinson, Bill "Bojangles," 73, 138n, 144-46
Rockwell, Tommy, 44
Rollini, Adrian, 90, 117
Rose, Billy, 99
Rough Riders, 11-12
Royal Garden Blues, 34, 53
Runnin' Wild, 51
Russell, Pee Wee, 88
Rusty Pail, 66
Rutherford, Anita, 58, 73, 85, 115, 133
Rutherford, Lewis, 47

St. Louis Blues, 80, 122-23
Sampson, Edgar, 8, 18
"San Juan Hill" (NYC), 11, 12
Santly, Joe, 52
Scandal in A Flat, 123-24
Schiffman, Frank, 72, 96
Schutt, Arthur, 111, 123
Scott, Hazel, 8
Sedric, Eugene "Honeybear," 36n, 45, 95-96, 135, 167
Senorita Mine, 75
Serenade for a Wealthy Widow, 85, 94
Shadow, The, 5
Shefter, Bert, 123
Shuffle Along, 23n, 72, 110
Shuffle Inn (NYC), 72
Sinatra, Frank, 8, 96
Sing an Old-Fashioned Song, 104
Singleton, Zutty, 88
'Sippi, 76
Sissle, Noble, 23n, 72
Slightly Less than Wonderful, 149-50, 157
Small's Paradise (NYC), 73
Smith, Bessie, 34, 51
Smith, Joe, 51, 60
Smith, Mamie, 35, 83, 84
Smith, Stuff, 158
Smith, Willie "The Lion," 6, 29, 30, 32, 33, 35, 37, 39, 40, 41-42, 51n, 57
Waller and, 34, 48, 91, 167
Solitude, 68, 159, 169
Sometimes I Feel like a Motherless Child, 2, 67-68, 120, 159, 169

Sousa, John Philip, 107-9
Southern Music Publishing Co., 36
Southern Suns, 95
"South Fifth Avenue" (NYC), 11, 12
Spanier, Muggsy, 52, 53, 81
Spargo, Tony, 117
Spreadin' Rhythm Around, 106-7
Squeeze Me, 2, 42, 43, 59, 85, 156n
Stevens, Ashton, 15
Stompin' at the Savoy, 8
Stormy Weather, 2, 9, 144-45
Stride music, 5-6, 26, 29-30
"Striver's Row" (NYC), 13, 60
"Studebaker Hour," 98
Sugar, 67
"Sugar Hill" (NYC), 13
Sweet Georgia Brown, 97
Sweet Savannah Sue, 43, 76, 87
Swing music, 123-24, 129, 133-34, 155
"Swing Street" (NYC), 8, 111

'Tain't Nobody's Business if I Do, 35, 36n
Tan Town Topics, 75
Tatum, Art, 110-11, 112, 156
Taylor, Eva, 34
Tea for Two, 156
Teagarden, Jack, 52, 53-54, 88
Ted Lewis & His Orchestra, 52
Ted Wallace and His Campus Boys, 117
That Ain't Right, 145
That Old Feeling, 120
That's the Way I Feel Today, 51
That's What I Like about You, 53-54
That's What the Bird Said to Me, 158
There's a Man in My Life, 149, 153, 157-58
There's Yes in the Air, 149, 158
They Won't Forget, 144
This Is So Nice, 149, 150, 157
Ticklers, 31-32
Tiger Rag, 59
Tin Pan Alley, 97, 98
Trambauer, Frank, 60, 61
Turner, Charlie, 104
Two Sleepy People, 157

Valentine, Hazel, 74
Valentine Stomp, 74

Venuti, Joe, 61n
Victor Records (Victor Talking Machine Company), 48, 56, 66, 69, 79-80, 84, 93, 95, 96, 102, 108, 113, 117, 129, 154, 156
Victor's #1 Hot Band, 84
Viper's Drag, 94-95
Vocalion Records, 44

Walker, Don, 153
Walker, George, 21
Waller, Edward Martin (father), 56, 57, 109, 155
Waller, Fats
   bands, 48, 49-50, 52
      His Rhythm, 5, 93-94, 95-96, 97, 98, 100-102, 103-4, 129, 140-41
      McKinney's Cotton Pickers, 51-52
      Morris' Hot Babies, 51
   broadway shows, 9, 62, 75-76, 147-54
   Carnegie Hall, 78, 135-39
   childhood, 14-19
   children, 36, 46, 56, 167
   compositions, 42-44, 48, 50, 52, 53, 57, 58-59, 60, 61, 63, 66, 76-78, 85, 97, 98, 125, 146, 153
   copyrights, 58, 62-63, 78, 107-8, 146
   death, 6-9, 62, 160-65
   drinking, 3-4, 6, 7, 43-44, 45-49, 54, 68, 74, 106, 116, 118, 125, 140, 165-166
   early career, 25, 38-40, 50
   eating, 3, 4, 61
   European tour, 115-21, 122-23, 125-26
   films, 2, 103, 106, 107, 144-47
   Gershwin and, 40-42
   greeting, 47
   Henderson and, 61, 63
   in Paris, 85-88
   Johnson and, 26, 27, 29, 32-34, 35, 39-40, 74, 110, 111, 135
   legal troubles, 57-58, 76, 113, 128, 131n
   marriages, 25, 36, 43, 55-56, 58, 133, 163
   Mitropoulos and, 139-40
   musical training, 18-19
   nickname, 33
   organist, 1, 2, 15, 65, 66-69, 86, 168-69

parents, 11, 14, 15-16, 17, 18, 26, 56, 57, 109, 155, 168
mother's death, 48, 55, 67, 112, 120, 168
radio, 4-5, 78, 80-81, 85, 88-90, 91, 93, 95, 129-35, 156, 160
recordings, 35, 36, 43, 48-50, 52-54, 56, 57, 59, 66, 67-68, 69-70, 80, 83, 84-85, 88, 93-94, 95, 96, 102, 103-4, 118-19, 125, 140-41, 154, 156
reissue, 105n
religion, 167-70
singing voice, 100
size, 47, 129
Smith and, 34, 37, 91
spirituals, 67-68, 119-20. 169
Tatum and, 110-11
television, 120
wit, 2-3, 47, 58, 68, 82, 85, 86, 118
Waller, Lawrence Robert (brother), 23, 24, 140, 169
Waller, Maurice (son), 121
Waller, Naomi (sister), 15, 17, 18, 24, 26, 27
Waller, Ronald (son), 46
Waller, Thomas, Jr. (son), 36, 56, 140
Waller Jive, 158
Washington, Dinah, 139
Waters, Ethel, 74, 109n
Welfare Island, 57
Welles, Orson, 18

Where Has My Mother Gone?, 168
Whispering, 69
White, Stanford, 12, 13
Whitechapel, 125-26
Whiteman, Paul, 41, 63, 69, 80, 91
WHN (radio station), 81
Wildcat Blues, 42
Wilkins, Barron D., 73-74
Williams, Bert, 21-22
Williams, Clarence, 34, 35, 42-43, 44, 81n
Williams, Mary Lou, 77, 111
Williams, Mrs. Harrison, 41-42
Williams, Spencer, 75, 85-87, 108, 119
Willow Tree, 76
Wilson, Teddy, 138
WLW (radio station), 88, 89, 95
WOR (radio station), 81
Wright, Mae, 121
Wright, Richard, 143
Wringin' and Twistin', 60, 61

Yamekraw, 78, 135
Yellow Dog Blues, 88
Yes Suh!, 88
Youmans, Vincent, 158
Young, Joseph, 103, 104
Your Feet's Too Big, 3

Ziegfeld Follies, The, 22
Zonky, 76